# LAKELAND HIKES
## Off the Beaten Track

## Doug Brown

SIGMA
*Leisure*

**Published by** Sigma Leisure – an imprint of
Sigma Press, 5 Alton Road, Wilmslow, Cheshire SK9 5DY, England.

**British Library Cataloguing in Publication Data**
A CIP record for this book is available from the British Library.

**ISBN:** 978-1-85058-843-6 (13-digit); 1-85058-843-0 (10-digit)

**Typesetting and Design by:** Sigma Press, Wilmslow, Cheshire.

**Cover photographs clockwise from top-left:** Pike de Bield; Crinkle Crags; Sunkenkirk Stone Circle; Helvellyn summit; Dale Head; Angle Tarn *(all by Doug Brown)*

**Maps and photographs:** Doug Brown

**Printed by:** Bell and Bain Ltd, Glasgow

**Disclaimer:** the information in this book is given in good faith and is believed to be correct at the time of publication. No responsibility is accepted by either the author or publisher for errors or omissions, or for any loss or injury howsoever caused. Only you can judge your own fitness, competence and experience. Do not rely solely on sketch maps for navigation: we strongly recommend the use of appropriate Ordnance Survey (or equivalent) maps.

# *Preface*

This book contains a selection of walks in Lakeland. The routes explore both remoter areas and less popular ways up the main hills and mountains. They are designed for people who enjoy the challenge of wandering off the beaten track and using their navigational skills for route finding and locating items of interest. Many map references are given to help navigation in poor visibility. Walkers with a GPS should enjoy the possibility of using this equipment to find precise locations.

Interesting natural features include tarns, waterfalls and crags associated with historical climbs. Man-made features include aircraft wrecks, old memorials, bothies, ancient dwelling places, hill forts, stone circles, mines and other industrial remains.

To give an idea of the bird life likely to be observed, I have mentioned those I have seen whilst completing these walks. For a little extra interest, I have also written about some of the people I have met.

The majority of the routes, all of which I completed in the period October 2005 to October 2006, are between 10km and 20km. They require a reasonable level of fitness and experience. On a clear day Lakeland provides lovely walks and following routes is not difficult. In adverse conditions, route finding can be a real challenge and getting lost may have serious consequences. Paths and slopes may become treacherous when icy or wet.

The routes often include the possibility of easy scrambles but these are easily avoided if conditions are poor. The lengths, total ascent and approximate times are given to help the reader determine the difficulty of each hike.

The walks are arranged in six sections:

❖ Central Lakeland

❖ Northern and North Western Lakeland

❖ Southern Lakeland

❖ Eastern Lakeland

- ❖ Western Lakeland
- ❖ Three Challenges

Two of the Three Challenges are longer and the reader is encouraged to vary the route according to their own preferences.

Where appropriate, information about mines is given. Inspections of the entrances are interesting but I would advise against further exploration unless accompanied by an expert.

An appendix with information and locations of over twenty aircraft wreck sites is included.

*Doug Brown*

# Contents

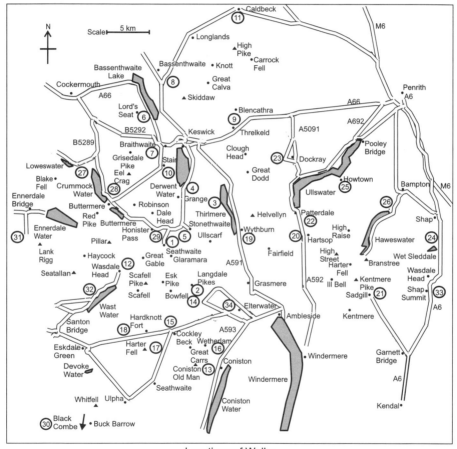

Locations of Walks

# Introduction

Lakeland is perfect for hill walking and a reasonably fit walker can climb any of the peaks in a single day. Many of the ridges are long so that once height is gained it is possible to maintain it. Their radial nature enables 'horseshoe' walks to be planned, starting and finishing in the same place. The region is large enough for a walker to find remote parts that see few visitors, yet compact enough for fell runners to cover all the main peaks in 24 hours. There are scrambles and rock climbs to suit all levels of ability. The moorland of the northern and eastern areas is similar to that of the Pennines and the Derbyshire Peak District. The area that was once the county of Westmorland tends to have gentler hills whilst the part that was formerly Cumberland is wilder and more remote. The walker is likely to experience a variety of conditions including snow, ice, rain, wind and sun (sometimes all in the same day!).

The views, with lakes in most valleys, distinctively shaped peaks, tarns, waterfalls and crags, are as beautiful as anywhere I have visited. Even early industry has failed to do great harm to the landscape, indeed, stone-axe factories, stone circles, ancient dwellings, mines, quarries etc. have added to the interest. A variety of birds may be found in the region with eagles and ospreys returning to breed in recent years. For the amateur geologist there is a wealth of rocks and minerals to investigate. In fact, it is difficult to see how the Lake District could be improved.

On a clear day, walking in Lakeland is an enjoyable, relaxing experience and navigation isn't difficult. In adverse conditions, route finding can be a real challenge and getting lost may have serious consequences.

When starting a walk or climb I tend to have negative thoughts, apprehensive about things that may go wrong. After a while, I feel more relaxed and often find myself smiling. I think this is due to a combination of physical exercise and the feeling of space and freedom. Even in rain and cloud, walking provides escape from everyday worries and there is the satisfaction of battling with the elements. There are days when one may as well start by standing in a stream to get over any futile attempts to keep one's feet dry.

This may sound silly, but I try to remember to thank each hill before I leave the summit. I hope these walks provide readers with interesting features to explore and enjoyable challenges to undertake.

## Early experiences

My first walking experience in the Lake District was on a camping trip with my friend, Jack, in our early teens. We pitched our tent in a field near the New Dungeon Ghyll Hotel in the Langdale valley. On our first day we got lost and returned soaked from Side Pike, less than 1km from the tent. On the second day, without a map, we ventured up the valley, followed other walkers and eventually found ourselves at the summit of Scafell Pike. My English teacher, G.G.W. of Lancaster Grammar School, happened to be sitting by the summit cairn. His only words were "Brown! Good God". A few years later, I did some easy rock climbing with another friend, Richard from Manchester University and I recall camping in Borrowdale, just after floods had made it a disaster area in 1966. Since then I have spent many days exploring the area.

## Distances and times

On many of the Lakeland paths it is possible to walk quite quickly. Over boggy or tussocky terrain progress is slower. Climbing uphill, scrambling or walking off-path also takes longer. When calculating the estimated times I have used an average speed of 3 km/h (2 mph), plus 90 minutes per 1000m of ascent and I have added more time for scrambles. (This is more generous than Naismith's rule of 3 mph + 30 minutes per 1000ft of ascent.) Speeds will be affected by weather and ground conditions, so the estimated times are only approximations.

## Parking

I have tried to start walks from places that have good car parking. Also, many of these points are on public transport routes.

## Scrambles

I have included some easy, Grade 1, scramble routes. These provide interesting ways to gain height. In normal conditions climbing equipment is not needed; in poor conditions they should be avoided. In most cases it is possible to bypass the scramble.

Brian Evans' books, *Scrambles in the Lake District North & South*, give further details and grades of scrambles. However, the level of difficulty will vary depending on how greasy the rock is. Hell Gill, Walk 14, is classed as Grade 1 but I feel this has a couple of more testing moves. 'Threading the Needle', an option in Walk 1, is classed as Grade 2, but I find it fairly straightforward.

## Maps

My maps are rough sketches. 1:25 000 Ordnance Survey maps are essential and should be referred to when planning a walk.

## Map references

A 6-figure reference covers a 100 metre square grid. Often more accuracy is needed, so for items such as aircraft wreck sites I have given a 10-figure reference. This implies accuracy to 1 metre, which is unrealistic, but it is usually accurate to within 10 metres. Mostly, I have given 10-figure references with the last figures as zero. This is to reflect possible errors but should be close enough to find the tops of hills. This also matches the format of 10 figures given by GPS readings.

To get the 6-figure reference from a 10-figure reference, simply take the first three figures from each half. For example: 12345/67890 becomes 123678.

The map references given in the book are readings from my GPS and should be reasonably accurate but please don't rely on them totally. Do check them on an OS map in case there is an error.

## Global Positioning System (GPS)

Many walkers now own a GPS. The ability to use a map and compass is essential but there are occasions, in poor conditions, when it is easy to become unsure of one's exact location. A basic GPS can give a very precise map reference. Also, looking for a particular point when in mist or cloud can be difficult and time consuming. My own experience, so far, is that the data given is very reliable, though there can be problems in obtaining accurate readings in gullies or by crags.

## Navigation

Most of these walks are designed for experienced walkers who are competent at map reading and in the use of a compass. When planning a walk there should be consideration of how to shorten a route or make it safer if the need arises. In poor visibility it is easy to become disorientated. Days may start perfectly clear but the weather can change rapidly. Ice and snow make even gentle slopes treacherous, and there are many crags and gullies that are too dangerous to attempt even in good conditions. Most valleys have some habitation but ones such as Eskdale and Langstrath are long, particularly when one is tired.

I have made many errors when navigating. When attempting the Lakes 3000'ers I managed to climb Scafell twice. More than once, I've ended up in Eskdale by mistake, including one occasion on Esk Pike, when my direction on leaving the summit was out by 180° (mental note; red is north on a compass, not black!). Another time, a group of us found ourselves halfway up St Sunday Crag when our objective had been Helvellyn, and that was in bright sunshine! The person at the front had simply followed footpath signs that led the wrong way, and the rest of us were too busy nattering to notice.

## Equipment

All the obvious, plus gaiters on boggy or heathery ground. Walking poles are useful for balance, crossing streams and for making descent easier on the knees. A torch is handy for looking inside the entrances of mines and caves. In winter conditions an ice axe and crampons should be used on steep slopes or on ice. In adversity, a sense of humour is extremely helpful!

## Wildlife

Various species of birds live on the fells and along the streams. Depending on the time of year these include: golden plovers, lapwings, curlews, short-eared owls, snow bunting, dotterel, dunlin, ring ouzels, wheatears, skylarks, meadow pipits, dippers, grey wagtails, grouse, kestrels, peregrines, buzzards, sparrow-hawks, ravens, merlins, ospreys and a rather lonely golden eagle. I have seen what I think was a male hen harrier. Red squirrels inhabit parts of the district and deer and fell-ponies live on the eastern fells. I have seen the occasional fox but haven't spotted one recently.

## Aircraft wrecks

Some of the routes go to the sites of aircraft wreckage, usually from World War Two. There are plaques at some of these sites, commemorating those who died. I feel it is fitting that more people should become aware of these aircrew who sacrificed their lives. Please respect these sites and do not remove any of the wreckage.

## Pubs

I have suggested a place for refreshment at the end of each walk. Even if you don't enjoy the routes, this book lists over 30 excellent pubs and inns. My apologies to any that I have overlooked.

## Names of places

I have tried to use the correct names but in many cases there is confusion. Books and maps often give different names. Is it Catbells or Cat Bells (Ordnance Survey), White Ghyll or White Gill, Mill Gill or Stickle Gill, Crag Hill or Eel Crag, Mirkiln Cove (OS) or Mirklin Cove and Fox Tarn (W. Heaton Cooper) or Foxes Tarn? Bowfell is often referred to as Bow Fell. Dore Head is Dove Head in Walt Unsworth's *The High Fells of Lakeland*. Names do evolve. Seventy years ago, Bagley named Brotherikeld (in Eskdale) as Butterilket (as does an old Ward Lock map). He also says that Esk Pike did not have an official name, and calls Ore Gap, Ewer Gap. Please forgive my transgressions.

## Reference Books

I have found these books very informative:

*The Pictorial Guides to the Lakeland Fells* – A. Wainwright.

A. H. Griffin's books about Lakeland and his Guardian Country Diary articles.

*The Tarns of Lakeland* – W. Heaton Cooper

*Complete Lakeland Fells* – Bill Birkett

*Mountain Lakeland* – Tom Bowker

*Beneath the Lakeland Fells* – Red Earth Publications

*Coniston Copper Mines, a Field Guide* – Eric Holland

*Scrambles in the Lake District* – Brian Evans

## Acknowledgements

Thanks to all those friends who have spent time walking or talking about the Lakeland with me. They include: Pete Booth, Phil Cassidy, Dave Clement, Owen Cooper, Robin Fletcher, Jan Gage, Adrian Greenwood, Bob Harrison, Chris Hill, Tony Hoyland, Peter Jones, Malcolm Keats, Bob Kissack, Jack Lee, Willie Lees, Chris Liles, Tony and Gerard Lyth, Mike Monaghan, Frank Murphy, Dave Richardson, Brian Rowntree, Richard Stevenson, Marilyn and Robert Tindall and Jake.

*Opposite: White Ghyll (Walk 2)*

# Section 1: Central Lakeland

# Walk 1. Great Gable from Seathwaite

**Maps:** OL4, OL6; map ref. prefix NY

**Distance:** 10km (6 miles)

**Ascent:** 880m (2900ft)

**Time:** 6 hours

**Starting point/parking:** Southern end of Borrowdale, at the end of the road to Seathwaite Farm (235123).

## General Description

This walk goes past waterfalls to Sty Head. The South Traverse of Great Gable is taken to the Great Napes region. Great Gable is climbed from the south. The route continues over Green Gable and down Gillercomb. There is the option of exploring the Borrowdale graphite mines. Most of the route is on paths. The way up Great Gable is by a scramble or up a steep scree slope. The classic climbs of Kern Knotts and Napes Needle are viewed. An aircraft wreck site may be visited.

## Route

As you walk through the farm at Seathwaite take a path on the right, through the buildings. Cross the footbridge over the stream. Don't take the path ahead that goes up by Sourmilk Gill. Instead, go through the gate on the left and follow the path beside the River Derwent. It isn't well defined at first, but becomes clearer after it passes through another gate in a fence, 400m away. Continue over boggy ground to a gate in a wall (230110). Through this, scramble up rocks, with views of Taylorgill Force that would be missed on the main path to Styhead Tarn. Continue on the west side of Styhead Gill to Styhead Tarn. Walk to the stretcher box at Sty Head (1).

The plan is to take the path that traverses across the screes, on the south side of Great Gable, to the Great Napes. From the stretcher box, start west along the path up Great Gable. After 20m take a path that branches left on a bearing of 260° (21870/09505). This leads to the South Traverse of Great Gable. Follow it to the climbing crag, Kern

Knotts (21530/09600). The face of the crag has two cracks graded Very Severe. The left one is Kern Knotts Crack (O.G. Jones was involved in the first ascent 1897). The right is Innominate Crack (Bentley Beetham 1921).

Go round the base of the crag and climb upwards to a path below a line of small crags (21350/09750). Continue to traverse across scree and boulders. A large scree shoot, Great Hell Gate, is met (21040/09900). Above, the rock climbing face of Tophet Wall is visible. Another patch of scree is reached (21000/09920). This also comes down from the side of Tophet Wall. More scree is crossed and Napes Needle comes into view, but is difficult to discern amongst the crags (2).

There is the opportunity of 'threading the Needle'. This is a very enjoyable Grade 2 scramble. To do this, 30m after the scree (20940/09910), climb towards a V-shaped groove that has light coloured rock on the upper half of the right side. Scramble up this groove to the back of Napes Needle. Descend the other side; there is an awkward step that needs care but overall this isn't a difficult route. If you don't 'thread the Needle' continue the traverse to Needle Gully (20890/09950), and

Author descending from Napes Needle

scramble up for a view of the Needle. It was first climbed by W. P. Haskett-Smith in 1886 (solo). I climbed it in about 1986! Getting up wasn't too bad but I didn't enjoy the descent. Opposite the Needle is an area known as the 'Dress Circle' because it gives an excellent view of climbers on the Needle. Continue west, either from the Dress Circle or on the path below. The next two patches of scree come together to the right of, and below Arrowhead Ridge. (Named because of the arrow-shaped rock, high above, on the end of the ridge.) The next ridge to the west is Sphinx Ridge and is easily recognised by the large rock at the front in the shape of the Sphinx.

Now, there are several options. The easiest way is to continue the traverse below Sphinx Ridge. A wide scree shoot is reached, Little

THE SCREES

YEWBARROW

MOSES'
FINGER

Wast Water from Great Gable

Hell Gate. This leads up towards the summit of Great Gable. I met a couple with three children, youngest 8 years old, who made mince-meat of Little Hell Gate. Another possibility is to continue past Little Hell Gate and scramble up the White Napes buttress, above the finger of rock known as Moses' Finger on Gavel Neese. My suggestion is a scramble that isn't too difficult, up the gully to the right (east) of Arrowhead Ridge. It is classed as Grade 2 if you end up on the ridge, but the suggested route is easier. Make your way up the grass and rock steps, between two scree shoots to a point directly below Arrowhead Ridge (approx. 20900/10000). This is level with the Sphinx on the next ridge. Move right towards the gully, Eagle's Nest Gully. To the right of a large, perched boulder is a second, smaller, perched boulder. Go right here, stepping across another lodged boulder, along a short, narrow ledge. It is now possible to enter the gully. Continue up the gully to a narrow, mossy rock step. Go back a couple of paces and bypass this on the left. Stay in the gully, without further difficulty, until there is an easy way up on the left.

A pleasant, grassy ridge is reached (20960/10125). Walk along this to Westmorland Crags (20995/10170). This short, rock face provides an enjoyable, easy scramble. Angle left, go right and then straight up on good holds. Continue by scrambling up the ridge on the left (21020/10225). Walk to Westmorland Cairn, above and to the right (21355/10230). Built in 1876 by the Westmorland Brothers; they considered it to be the finest viewpoint in the Lake District. From the cairn, walk easily uphill to Great Gable summit (21100/10320, elevation 899m (2949ft)) (3).

Notice the plaque just to the north of the cairn. This is The Fell and Rock Climbing Club's memorial to their members who died in World War 1. From Great Gable take the path NE. This descends steeply to Windy Gap. Go across the gap and up to the summit cairn of Green Gable (21470/10710, elevation 801m (2628ft)) (4). A small amount of wreckage, from the crash of an Anson, a trainer aircraft, lies 50m from the summit on a bearing of 150° (21497/10663). There are a few more pieces a little further down the mountain. The two airmen were killed.

Leave the summit NE and swing to a bearing of 060°, following the cairns marking the path to Base Brown. Take the path that branches left (22000/11050). This drops down to Gillercomb Head. It is a good path, in a lovely setting above Sourmilk Gill, and goes round the west side of Base Brown to the top of the waterfalls. A steep path by the side of the gill, as is plunges towards Seathwaite, gives good views of the falls.

For an alternative route that explores old graphite mines, cross the gill above the top waterfall (227122) (5). Contour northwards for 700m to a wall above the mines.

The Borrowdale mines were the only source of graphite (black-lead, wad or plumbago) in the Lake District. The mineral, discovered by farmers, was first used to mark sheep. The Cumberland Pencil Factory was founded using this material. It was based in Braithwaite initially but moved to Keswick. This black mineral was so valuable that it was often stolen, leading to the term 'black market'.

There are various workings down the hillside near Newhouse Gill. Above the wall at the top of the fell there is a quarry (23030/12800). Climb a stile over the wall near the gill. There are more mine work-

ings below the wall. By a holly tree there is a deep shaft
(23150/12700). Below is a horizontal entrance that the brave may
walk into to see the shaft and tunnels. A rope by the shaft indicates
that experts explore here. Ruined mine entrances, open shafts and
tunnels are along the spoil heaps as you drop down the hillside.
There are two tunnels by north bank of the gill (23090/12720 &
23140/12650). Signs say 'DANGER DEEP EXCAVATIONS'. The drier
tunnel has a shaft about 15m from the entrance. (It wasn't the author
who ventured in; he just sheltered from the rain, in the entrance).
Between these tunnels is a small dam. There is a ruined building, a
guardhouse, and a tunnel with a low entrance (23290/12610).

The Borrowdale Yews, marked on OS maps, are by a stream at the
bottom of the hill. One tree, 40m above the path to Seatoller, has a
fence round it. A plaque commemorates the Queen's Jubilee in 2002.
It says 'This yew has been selected as one of fifty Great Britain trees by
the Tree Council.'

Wordsworth wrote a poem, *Yew Trees*, which included these lines:

> 'But worthier still of note
> Are those Fraternal Four of Borrowdale
> Joined in one solemn and capacious grove.'

(Three of the trees are still there).

A path goes along the riverbank to the farm at Seathwaite. On the
path, a new stone commemorates John Bankes, a former owner of the
Seathwaite Wad Mine. It replaces an older stone 'WILFULLY
DESTROYED'.

On the way back towards Keswick, the Scafell Hotel in Rosthwaite
has a public bar with a good fire in winter.

# Walk 2. High Raise from Great Langdale

**Map:** OL6; map ref. prefix NY

**Distance:** 13.5km (8.5 miles)

**Ascent:** 1100m (3600ft)

**Time:** 6¾ hours

**Starting point/parking:** There are two car parks near the New Dungeon Ghyll Hotel; free to NT Members (294064).

## General Description

This walk visits the less frequented White Ghyll on the way to Pavey Ark. It then goes to Sergeant Man, High Raise and the various tops around the Langdale Pikes. There is the possibility of descending alongside Dungeon Ghyll, this requires care and is best avoided in poor conditions. Some of the route is off-path but not over difficult terrain. A little scrambling is possible. Stone-axe sites and rock climbing areas are visited.

## Route

Walk past the New Hotel to a gate by Stickle Cottage. After 30m go right and cross a footbridge over Stickle Ghyll (Mill Gill). Go uphill by the stream for 100m to a gate on the right and take a path alongside a wall (29430/06690). After 300m, White Ghyll is reached (29730/06800) (1). Go up it, either by the stream bed or a path on the right. The walls to the right have several rock climbs including Jim Birkett's 1947 Slip Knot (Not), Do Not, Haste Not, Perhaps Not and Joe Brown's Laugh Not. The latter is on the Lower Crag just before the large sycamore. It goes up a thin crack in a reddish corner; the rock to the left has a black patch and the climb finishes by an overhang. The climbing area of the Upper Crag is above the sycamore.

Use the larger boulders for the easiest way up the gill. Continue past a small waterfall to the open fells (29710/07390). Walk to the top of the gill, then make your way past a boggy area, on a bearing of approximately 300°, towards Pavey Ark, which soon comes into

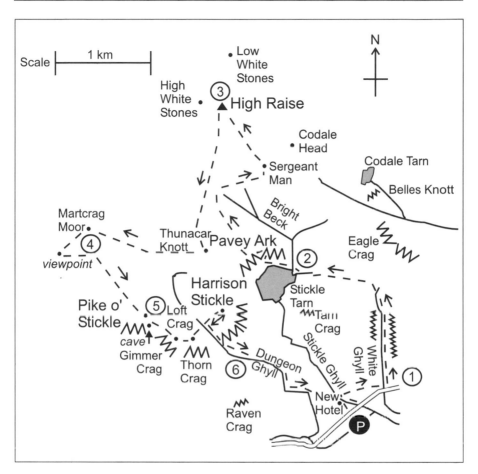

view. (I saw wheatears and meadow pipits around here.) The main path round Stickle Tarn to Pavey Ark is joined. It is better to use the grassy steps and boulders to the right of the path to get to the foot of Jake's Rake (2).

If you've been up Jake's Rake, for a change I suggest you try Easy Gully. The start is at 28600/07910. There is one tricky bit, where the easiest way is to the left of the centre, right of a jutting-out rock. The main path up the east side of Pavey Ark is near but 10m before this, make your way up grassy ledges and large boulders to the summit cairn (28450/07900, elevation 697m, (2288ft)).

The next target is Sergeant Man, 1km away. Go left of north, contouring round to the top of Bright Beck where a faint path is reached (28100/08610). Continue on this until you are below Sergeant Man (28600/08730). Then make your way to the lowest point of the crag. This gives easy scrambling on good rock to the top (28640/08900, elevation 736m (2414ft)).

Take a path NW for 800m to the trig point and shelter on High Raise (28080/09540, elevation 762m (2500ft)) (3). From here, go southwards on the path to Thunacar Knott, 1.5km away. There is a cairn to the north of the summit and one at the summit (27970/07990, elevation 723m (2372ft)).

Martcrag Moor is worth a visit because it was a chipping site for stone axes. To get there, aim west for 1km. As you drop down, a good path is met that goes to the moor. This area is covered with boggy peat and I didn't find any evidence of stone-axe making, though there is a good viewpoint and cairn at the edge above the valley (26465/08000) (4). From here, go due east to the main path to the Langdale Pikes and walk uphill to Pike o'Stickle. Scramble up the west side to the summit (27400/07360, elevation 709m (2324ft)) (5). From the top another popular climbing area, Gimmer Crag, may be seen below Loft Crag.

The scree slope to the east of Pike o'Stickle is well known as the location of a stone-axe factory. Just over 100m down the scree, on the right, is a man-made cave where there was a vein of suitably hard rock. The scree is very loose but with care it is possible to visit the cave. The scree chute used to give a very fast descent to the valley floor. Once, years ago, I struggled all the way down carrying a large, reluctant 'Dulux' dog.

Back at the top of the chute, go east over Loft Crag (27740/07130, elevation 682m (2238ft)) and Thorn Crag (28000/07130, elevation 642m (2106ft)). Cross the top of Dungeon Ghyll and, using rocks where possible, scramble up to the summit of Harrison Stickle (28170/07380, elevation 736m (2414ft)). Return to the path by the side of Dungeon Ghyll. It is possible to inspect the top of the ghyll but a waterfall soon forces you out. Past the first fall you may again drop into the ghyll but a narrow gorge and fall are impassable. Return to the main path until the slope eases and then leave it to go down to the ghyll (28220/07060) (6).

Walk by the side of the water to two rowan trees above a fine water-

Easy Gully

fall (28530/06900). There is a way to regain the gorge below the fall but it involves descending a short, steep section near the bottom of the gorge. I wouldn't recommend it in wet or icy conditions. Above the fall, go to the right for 100m, climbing slightly, to get to the other side of a reddish, loose gully. Descend the grass slope to a steep section (28600/06880). You should be level with scree on the far side of Dungeon Ghyll. Angle back, towards the fall, on a narrow ledge. This leads to a small rowan tree growing sideways out of the bank. The tricky bit is sliding down a rock for the last four feet. Having done this, you are rewarded with good views of the waterfall and further progress down the ghyll is possible. (If you wish to avoid the ghyll, go SW from the top of the waterfall to pick a path that leads above Raven Crag and down to the New DG Hotel).

Below the waterfall there are more cascades and falls. Make your way through large boulders on the right bank until the stream narrows. On the left side step up two metres, on reddish rock, to a narrow path. This descends steeply and is loose, so take care. An attractive 25ft waterfall is followed by a 40ft water slide. This is a beautiful area that many people never see. Where the water reaches a narrow gorge take a path on the right, through bracken, to a main path. There is one final treat. Look for a path to the left (29000/06570). This leads to a natural bridge, formed by boulders, over the ghyll. With care, it is possible to climb across. Below, there is a view of a dark, sinister gorge and another waterfall. It is possible to enter the ghyll lower down and walk back for a better view of this lower fall. Continue along the side of the ghyll to a footbridge. Cross it and walk to a gate on the left. The path leads back to the New DG Hotel and the Sticklebarn Tavern.

### *Note:*

Martcrag Moor is a site where suitable stones were chipped to make axes. In the 1920s a Professor Watson found axe heads in the peat on the moor. A Mr Bunch of Ulverston discovered the stone-axe factory by Pike o'Stickle in 1947. After chipping, the axes were taken to Beckermet on the coast, which had sandstone for the final polishing process.

# Walk 3. High Seat and Ullscarf from Thirlmere

**Map:** OL4; map ref. prefix NY

**Distance:** 19.5km (12 miles)

**Ascent:** 1020m (3350ft)

**Time:** 8½ hours

**Starting point/parking:** Take the minor road round the west side of Thirl-mere, off the A591 Ambleside to Keswick road. There are two car parks at Armboth, 2km from the north end of the lake (306170). The one to the west of the road is free.

## General Description

Middlesteads Gill provides an easy scramble onto the fells. The route goes over open ground to the north of Bleaberry Fell and turns south, along the main ridge over High Seat to Ullscarf. It returns over open ground to Armboth Fell and descends alongside Fisher Gill. Over half this walk is on paths but the area is one of the boggiest in the Lakes. The best time is when the ground is frozen; next best is after a long, dry spell. I did this walk in January on a perfect winter's day, sunny with no wind. The ground was icy in places and there was snow on Ullscarf. If time is pressing the walk can be curtailed at High Tove.

## Route

Walk north along the road, to the stile on the left. This is the start of the footpath that goes up by Fisher Gill. Through the stile is a bridge over Middlesteads Gill. The gill, a Grade 1 scramble, is in a delightful setting. The ravine is narrow and provides a lovely way to gain height. It isn't daunting and it is easy to escape. On the day I describe there was ice in the gill and some of the rocks were glazed but it was mainly dry, with firm footing.

The first part of the stream is simply boulder-hopping. A ravine is reached with a very short enclosed part; bridging across the sides will keep your feet dry. A water slide bars the way ahead. It is usually possible to bypass this on the right and regain the stream bed above the fall but I found the rocks too icy and had to retreat a few steps to escape up the left bank. I got back into the ravine above the icy part. A jammed boulder is met and passed by a narrow, easy ledge on the left. Proceed past a dead tree to a cascade that is climbed on the left. A tree trunk lies across the stream and the end of the ravine is reached. Climb up the grassy bank on the left, to the open fell-side and magnificent views (1).

Go north to the deer fence surrounding the forest. Follow the fence uphill and continue northwards on sheep tracks above the fence. 800m from Middlesteads Gill, go to a cairn, 150m from the fence (29800/17830). To the north, 800m from this cairn, is another cairn on a rocky knoll, with two standing stones below. Walk across open ground to these (29575/18590).

One stone has a brass plate inscribed "In

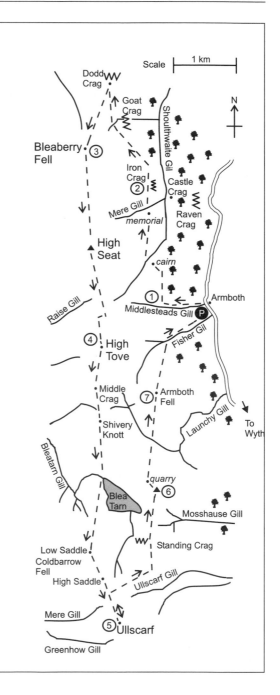

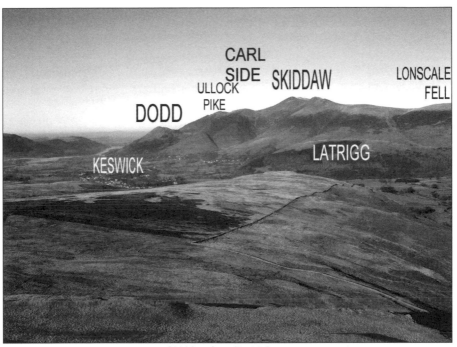

Skiddaw from Dodd Crag

memory of J. Litt who died March 9 1880". The writing on the other post is difficult to interpret, but I could make out some of the words:

> WE FOUND THIS STONE
> IN MERE GILL AND
> PLACED IT HERE.....
>
> ...........................
> .....   TO MARK THE
> SPOT WHERE HIS
> SPIRIT FLED TO THE
> GLORIOUS HOME ....
>
> ...........................

Opposite the knoll, surrounded by fir trees, is Raven Crag, a rock climbing area. You should be able to pick out the site of a hill fort on Castle Crag, 500m away.

Continue north for 600m over Mere Gill to Iron Crag (29620/19210), enjoying the views to the east. There aren't any paths but sheep tracks provide some help (2). Next walk 600m, bearing 325° to Goat Crag, rising gradually over rough ground. By looking over the edge it is possible to get a glimpse of the vertical cliffs of the crag, another climbing area. Walk northwards along the edge. (When you drive along the A591, Iron Crag, Raven Crag and Goat Crag may be seen clearly and their climbing potential appreciated.)

Although it is possible to make directly for Bleaberry Fell, it is worth going 700m further north to Dodd Crag. Go NW below a small crag to a fence and climb over a stile. Walk along the top of the fell to Dodd Crag, no cairn, with views of Blencathra, Skiddaw, and Bassenthwaite Lake. On the way, a wall has to be crossed and there isn't a stile. Turn back and pick up the fence on your left. This leads all the way to Bleaberry Fell. The wall is crossed again, this time next to a gate. Go to the top of Bleaberry Fell, with its cairn(s) and shelter (28570/19570, elevation 590m (1935ft)) (3). A girl reached the cairn before me and added a stone. Her mother arrived and said that she was collecting Wainwrights and had 68 to go.

Follow the main ridge south for 1.5km, along a fence, to the cairn and trig point on High Seat, (28710/18050, elevation 608m (1995ft)). Keep on the path to High Tove for a further 1.5km (28910/16510, elevation 515m (1689ft)) (4). After rain this ridge will be very boggy but on that day most of the ground was frozen.

If you are ready to call it a day, a path from Watendlath crosses High Tove and leads back to Armboth. Those with the time and energy may continue on the main path for another 2km over Middle Crag, Shivery Man and Shivery Knott to Blea Tarn. As you near it, leave the main path and keep to the west side of the tarn. In January, this was frozen over with a thin sheet of ice. Climb the shoulder to the west of the tarn, to Coldbarrow Fell, and visit Low Saddle (28810/13300) and High Saddle (28930/12920). The fell climbs gradually to Ullscarf (29150/12170, elevation 726m (2382ft)) (5). Near the top, a small patch of ice covered by snow caught me out and I suffered my first fall of the day.

The objective is to return north along the eastern side of the moor. Follow the path along the fence for 1.5km to Standing Crag. At the bottom of the crag, leave the path and aim for a trig point on a knoll, 500m to the north (29830/14300) (6). Just below here are old mine workings and a neat, walled structure. Drop down to the north, curving round marshy ground at the top of Launchy Gill. Climb a stile over a fence (29560/14860). Go along a track past a ruined wall and climb gradually towards Armboth Fell, aiming for a boulder perched on the horizon. A rocky knoll is ahead but there is a higher point 250m to the NE. This is the top of Armboth Fell (29680/15970, elevation 479m (1570ft)) (7). Some people consider this to be the centre of the Lake District.

Keep north for 600m and cross Fisher Gill. A few metres away, on the north side of the gill, a path goes down steeply to Armboth, past a large boulder perched in a precarious fashion near the road.

The King's Head Hotel is the nearest inn, on the other side of Thirlmere at the foot of Helvellyn.

### Note:

Thirlmere Reservoir was opened in 1894. The aqueduct carries 200 million litres of water to the Manchester area each day, at about 4mph and falling 50cm (20 inches) per mile without pumps. It goes through a four mile tunnel under Dunmail Raise.

# Walk 4. The Jaws of Borrowdale

**Map:** OL4; map ref. prefix NY

**Distance:** 20km (12.5 miles)

**Ascent:** 1090m (3600ft)

**Time:** 8½ hours

**Starting point/parking:** In Grange, by the bridge (253175). Alternatively, by the B5289, north of the turn to Grange (256176), or south of the turn (253174).

## General Description

From Grange the route goes over Castle Crag to Rosthwaite. The return is over Great Crag, Grange Fell and Brown Dodd. There are visits to Millican Dalton's caves, and memorials to King Edward VII and the men of Borrowdale who died in the Great War. For the most part the route is on good paths. Where the suggested way is over open ground, it is often possible to find faint paths. The summits are relatively low, which makes this walk a good choice for a day when the higher peaks are in cloud. The views of Borrowdale, Derwent Water, and Skiddaw are delightful.

## Route

Starting in Grange, walk west and take the sign-posted footpath on the left, just past the café. This leads to the campsite at Hollows Farm. (In January, we saw two woodpeckers in the woods and two herons on the marshy ground.) Don't go to the farm but turn left on the track that leads past the campsite to Castle Crag. (A dipper flew across the river and a goldcrest was performing acrobatics in the trees by the water.) Cross over a stream (there is a bridge) and take a left fork into Low Hows Wood. Go to a junction at the top of a rise in the woods, by a signpost for 'Rosthwaite' and 'Grange' (25180/16070). Turn right, along a mine track off the main path, bearing 240°. This winds uphill to caves made by slate quarrying. The first cave usually has a wet floor but the second is where Millican Dalton spent many summers in the first half of the 20th century. This self-styled 'Professor of Adventure', was a member of The Fell and Rock Club, a rock climber and also sailed rafts in the area. The cave has a higher compartment, the bedroom cave, which has its own entrance. On its left side, as you enter, chiselled in the slate is "DON'T WASTE WORDS". Below is added "JUMP TO CONCLUSIONS".

From the cave, return to the main path that goes to the east of Castle Crag and walk along this towards Rosthwaite. 200m after you emerge from the wood go through a gate on the right (252153). A path goes up the hill past spoil heaps and close to a small shelter. It continues, through a wall, to meet paths from the west and south. Go over a stile, to the bottom of a spoil heap and take the track that zigzags steeply up it to a quarry, where there is a sculpture park formed from pieces of slate. A path on the right goes to the summit of Castle Crag (1). There is a war memorial on the summit rock. The first name on the list is John Hamer who was killed on 22 March 1918. His father gave the crag to the National Trust in 1920.

From Castle Crag our next objective is Rosthwaite. Take the zigzag path south, down the spoil heap. At the bottom take a path heading south. This leads to the main path to Rosthwaite, crossing the River Derwent at New Bridge. In Rosthwaite, by the shop, turn left along the main valley road (2). Outside the village, turn right and cross the bridge over Stonethwaite Beck. (To the left, is a camping barn called Dinas Hoggus. I stayed there in February 2006 and met a father and son, Hugh and Austin. Hugh had done the Coast to Coast Walk 38 times, mainly guiding groups. By summer 2006 he expected the total to reach 40.)

Turn right and walk along a track towards Stonethwaite. Keep to the east side of Stonethwaite Beck and, 200m after the bridge to Stonethwaite fork left to climb on a good path, through the woods (265137) (3). At the top, above the wood, there is the option of visiting two minor tops, White Crag and Knotts. White Crag is a short climb to the NW. Then, to get to Knotts carry on NW, squeezing past the end of a wall on the right side. Return below White Crag, over a ruined wall, to join the path to Dock Tarn (4). This tarn is set in beautiful scenery. Go along the west shore and for a good view of the tarn, scramble up a rocky outcrop to the north. Go 400m NW to the top of Great Crag; there are various paths to choose from. There are two tops, 80m apart (27000/14760 and 27000/14680). I think the southern top is slightly higher.

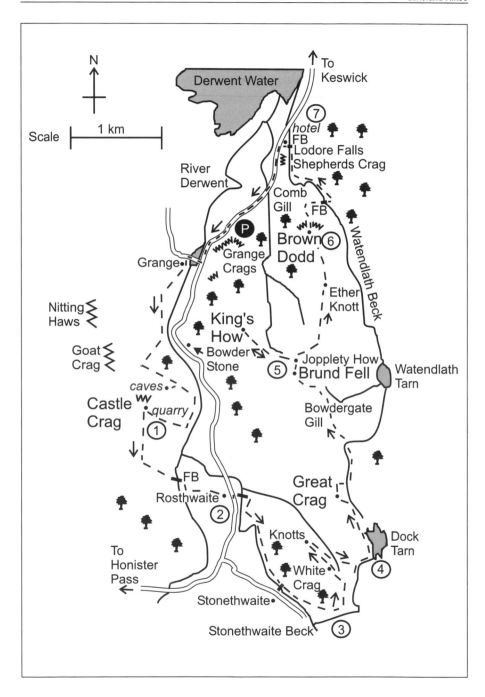

CATBELLS SKIDDAW

Derwent Water from King's How

Now, go to the east of north dropping down through crags to a wall. Follow this, right, to a gate and the main path. This takes you to the east of flat, boggy ground. A sign at the far side requests walkers to avoid this wetland. The path goes to a wall and a gate, by a stream (270155). Through the gate, follow the path northwards to Puddingstone Bank.

Cross the main Rosthwaite to Watendlath path and go through a gate in the wall ahead. Climb over a stile on the left and use sheep tracks to get to Brund Fell (26410/16240) (5). There is a second, lower peak 60m to the NE. Go NE for 100m, scramble up Jopplety How, (26550/16370), and down the north side to a wall.

A diversion may be made to visit King's How, although you may prefer to leave it for another day. To get there, turn west at the wall and follow it for 400m to a stile. From here a path leads NW to King's How (25810/16640). The views of Derwent Water and the surrounding hills are superb. On the north face of the summit, by a path, is a memorial to King Edward VII, dedicated by his sister, Louise.

From King's How, return to the wall north of Jopplety How and find a wall that runs north over Joppletyhow Moss. Take a path that passes to the west side of Ether Knott and turn back to climb up to the summit (26830/17160). Various sheep tracks lead, through heather, to Brown Dodd (26600/17710) (6). (I saw ravens and a buzzard along here.) Keep slightly right of north, descending through crags, in the direction of Derwent Water. A steep path drops down, with a silver birch tree giving a good foothold (26533/17818). There is a rocky prominence with views of Derwent Water and Bassenthwaite (26560/17900).

A path leads to a gate in a wall by Ladder Brow (26570/18150). To the left a path goes to High Lodore but it is more interesting to turn right (east). Walk 300m to a footbridge over Watendlath Beck. Cross it and go through a gate in the wall on the left. Leave the main path, and take one close to the stream; this can be followed all the way, past spectacular waterfalls, to the hotel at the bottom. You may get poetic urges! In places, trees have fallen across the path otherwise there are no difficulties. Cross the footbridge behind the hotel, where there is a slot in the wall for donations! (7) Turn left along the road back to Grange.

The public bar of the Scafell Hotel in Rosthwaite has a board listing the winners of the annual Borrowdale Fell Race. The race starts and finishes in Rosthwaite, and goes to Bessyboot, Scafell Pike, Great Gable and Dale Head. The record time is 2 hours 34 minutes 38 seconds by Billy Bland in 1981.

### Note:

A friend, Frank Murphy, met Millican Dalton a few times. One tip he got from him was to partly undo some of the screws on the soles of his boots to get a better grip on icy rock. Millican also talked to Frank about a trip to Monte Rosa. Frank was a member of the Achille Ratti Climbing Club and the 1946 club journal has Frank's description of the E Route climb on Gimmer Crag.

# Walk 5. Glaramara and Scafell Pike from Stonethwaite

**Maps:** OL4, OL6; map ref. prefix NY

**Distance:** 22km (13.5 miles)

**Ascent:** 1600m (5250ft)

**Time:** 10 hours

**Starting point/parking:** By the lane to Stonethwaite (259139) or by the phone-box in Stonethwaite (262137).

## General Description

This route explores the Borrowdale Fells between the Seathwaite and Langstrath valleys. It may be extended to Scafell Pike. The return is along the quiet Langstrath valley. Most of the walk is on good paths. The minor tops of the Borrowdale Fells are confusing in cloud, so it is best to choose a day when the lower fells are clear. An aircraft crash site lies close to the route. In Ian McEwan's novel, *Amsterdam*, one of his characters does a walk over some of the same ground but in the opposite direction: starting along Langstrath, then returning over Allen Crags and Thornythwaite Fell. The annual Borrowdale Fell Race, held on the first Saturday in August, starts in Rosthwaite, goes to Bessyboot and along some of this route to Scafell Pike (see Walk 4).

## Route

Starting from Stonethwaite, walk along a stony lane to the campsite. Opposite the entrance to the campsite is a green, metal gate (266133). Go through this, to a path on the left side of Big Stanger Gill. This rises through the trees, with man-made steps in places. Above the wood, follow the gill to a small waterfall between two silver birch trees; to the left of the fall is the possibility of a short scramble. Continue along the right side of the gill. The first target, Bessyboot, lies along the third ridge on the left. Leave the gill (25940/12750), go SW for 200m and then south to the cairn on Bessyboot (25840/12490, elevation 550m (1807ft)) (1).

Head south on a path that passes Tarn at Leaves on the west side.

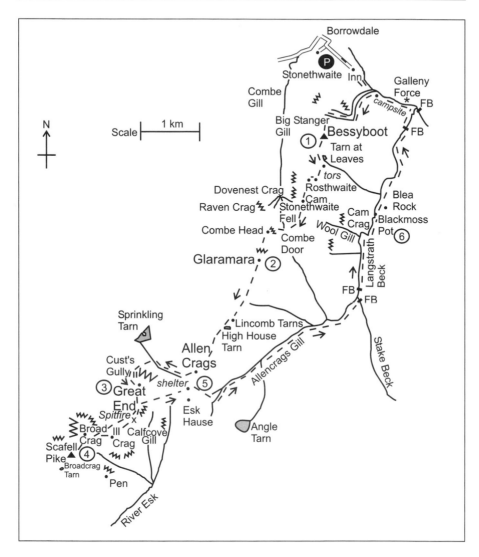

Scramble up a rocky tor, 200m south of the tarn. Go another 200m on 200° to another tor, then 100m west to the prominent tor of Rosthwaite Cam (25580/11820, elevation 612m (2008ft)). I scrambled up the east side, to the left of an overhang. On the opposite side of Combe Gill is a good view of Raven Crag, one of the areas where the legendary O.G. Jones climbed. A pleasant aspect of these fells is that the actual distances are shorter than they seem.

RED PIKE

GREAT GABLE

GREEN GABLE

YEWBARROW

The view from Allen Crags

Continue south across the Great Hollow (not so great!). A line of rocks, by a pool, leads to a small crag (25630/11530). Scramble up this to the cairn on Stonethwaite Fell (25650/11400, elevation 632m (2073ft)). Below here are Doves Nest Caves, worth visiting on another day.

Head 200° across lower ground, past pools, to a crag 450m away. Go up this, then west, down to the gap of Combe Door. A rock face bars the way to Combe Head. Go right, to the northern end, scramble up, starting leftwards, and then go across to the cairn on Combe Head (24950/10940, elevation 733m (2405ft)). There are views of Combe Gill and the Borrowdale Fells you traversed earlier. Go SW, by pools, to join the path and the short scramble up Glaramara. There are two cairns, 25m apart. The higher is by a shelter (24720/10560, elevation 783m (2568ft)) (2).

Go southwards over a minor bump (the main path misses this to the west). Drop down and join the path to Allen Crags. Along here are several lovely tarns including High House Tarn and Lincomb Tarns.

One especially pretty tarn is placed between rocky tors (24050/09280). For a spot of fun, traverse the rock face on the east side of the tarn, just above the water. This tarn, or the smaller one just to the south may be the fictional location of an attack on a woman in Ian McEwan's novel. Continue southwards to Allen Crags (23670/08520, elevation 785m (2574ft)). Drop down to the crossroads to the south (23480/08320). If it's cold and you want to rest, walk 75m to the popular shelter below Esk Hause.

One option is to head for the Langstrath valley and omit Scafell Pike altogether. Another is to take the main path over the flank of Great End to Scafell Pike. My suggestion is to go to the western end of the north face of Great End to view the jammed rock in Cust's Gully. This involves the loss of about 100m in height.

Near here in October 2006, Jan and I chatted to three men, Ian, Gwyn and Steve, who do the magnificent work of repairing eroded footpaths. They explained they were the Western Valleys team, one of four in the Lakes, and that on an average day they create about 4m of path. They work a 10-hour day, including walking to and from their base in Wasdale. A few minutes after we left them, they had nipped across to the slopes of Green Gable where they seemed to be selecting suitable rocks for their work.

Take the path NW towards Sprinkling Tarn. Opposite the gullies of Great End leave the path (229087). Climb diagonally westwards below the north buttress of Great End. (There is a good view of Central Gully; a difficult scramble in summer but it's a good crampon climb in winter conditions). The best way up is to the left of a dry gully, to the right of scree. Cross the gully to avoid a mossy boulder. Go up to a point where two gullies start (22590/08630). The gully on the right is repulsively mossy. The one to the left is Cust's Gully and is easily recognised by a jammed boulder. The boulder is the sight you came to see but I would avoid the gully, a nasty, Grade 2 scramble. It is very mossy and loose. I went up the stairway on the left side beneath the jammed boulder. The last move at the top of the stairway is awkward to say the least; I think I closed my eyes! After passing under a lower chockstone you think it's all over, but there is a sting in the tail. The last part is a green, wet, mossy chimney. I found a hold for my left hand and water poured down my armpit. The key is a step, high up, for the right foot.

Author, Lincomb Tarns

To avoid this misery, go 20m right from the bottom of the two gullies. Walk up a grassy tongue and scramble up easily for 8m (22570/08640). There are crampon marks on the rocks – made by sensible people who have rejected Cust's Gully.

Cross scree and go up the steep grass slope, past the top of the right-hand gully, to the top of Cust's Gully.

Go SW to a cairn not far from the top. I think the view from here is as good as any in the Lakes. Walk across to the Great End summit cairn (22530/08460, elevation 910m (2984ft)) (3). (If you drop down a short distance to the SW, you will see a pretty tarn below, Lambfoot Dub; as its name implies, it's shaped like a lamb's foot.) Walk southwards to join the main Scafell Pike path (the M1). A short detour right goes to the top of Broad Crag. Continue to Scafell Pike (21540/07230, elevation 978m (3210ft)) (4)

Return along the M1 past Broad Crag and this time visit the top of Ill Crag (22310/07350, elevation 935m (3067ft)). Go north along the eastern edge of Ill Crag. 130m below the M1, is a small amount of wreckage from a Spitfire that crashed in 1947. A memorial plaque for the pilot is attached to a nearby rock (22505/07714). Continue eastwards, along the M1, to the shelter below Esk Hause (5).

Walk along the path for 400m, in the direction of Angle Tarn, to where the path crosses Allencrags Gill (23900/08100). Drop down steeply on the east side of the beck. A large boulder is reached and, 50m below this, it is possible to enter the gorge. Step down to the left; on the far side of the gill (and slightly lower), is a vertical wall that has a large black patch. The gorge opens up and there are no difficulties going along it. An area is reached where holly, rowan, silver birch and pools of water form a lovely spot. Notice how the trees have grown out of crevices that sheep can't reach. The stream becomes Langstrath Beck and there are paths on both sides. A waterfall and pool, Blackmoss Pot (Blackmer Pot), make an attractive scene (6). A large boulder, Blea Rock, the size of a house, is 300m further on. There seems to be one relatively easy way up, but even that would require climbing equipment.

If you are on the east bank, cross to the west at a footbridge (271126). Admire the waterfall of Galleny Force; then go through the nearby gate. Follow the path through the campsite and fields to the Langstrath Country Inn, which should not be missed. It has old photographs and a 1927 poster, advertising midnight walks up Skiddaw, 3 shillings, also climbing in Doves Nest Caves, £2 2s. The beers included 'Crag Rat' and 'Doris' 90th Birthday Ale'! In Ian McEwan's novel, a character stays at a hotel in Stonethwaite. As there is only one, I presume that this is it, though I didn't see a fox in a glass case! I think I recall that when custom was slack during the foot and mouth troubles, the landlord manned a boot dipping post near the inn.

*Opposite: Goldscope Mine (Walk 10)*

# Section 2: Northern and North Western Lakeland

# Walk 6. Lord's Seat and Whinlatter from Powter How

**Map:** OL4; map ref. prefix NY

**Distance:** 10.5km (6.5 miles)

**Ascent:** 650m (2130ft)

**Time:** 5 hours

**Starting point/parking:** Car park at Powter How, by minor road off A66 at the southern end of Bassenthwaite Lake (220265).

## General Description

This walk starts over Barf to Lord's Seat. It continues to Whinlatter and then down to the Forestry Commission Visitors Centre. It returns along Comb Beck and through Thornthwaite. The route begins steeply, up scree, past a rock known as the 'Bishop' followed by a short scramble on the way to Barf. (There is an alternative path by

The Bishop

Beckstones Gill.) After the initial ascent the walk is mainly on good paths and through forest. Jan and I did this walk on a cold, winter's day.

## Route

From the car park cross the road, past what was once the Swan Hotel and take the wide track on the right. Go through the gate to a standing rock that is painted white, this is the 'Clerk'. Above this, there is a larger rock, also painted white, the 'Bishop'. To reach the Bishop it is better to go a few metres past the Clerk and take a slightly less direct route up the loose scree (1). (Jan avoided the scree and the scramble above, by taking the path along the southern side of Beckstones Gill to the top of Barf.) Behind the Bishop, go up the obvious gully to a rowan tree with the initials KKG carved on the trunk. Follow a thin path up, to the middle of a crag. From near the centre, a rake angles across the crag to the left edge. Take this but be careful, there is one awkward

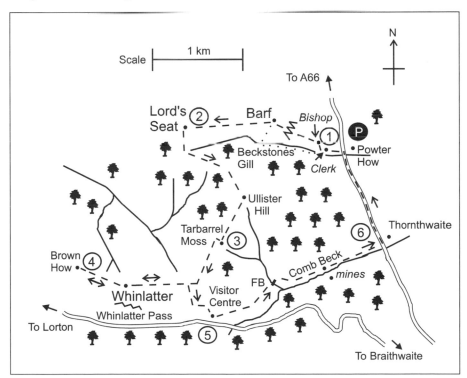

step. A path continues left, to a tree. Then, turn back to the right and scramble up the ridge above the crag. Follow the path overlooking Bassenthwaite Lake and go up easy ground to the summit of Barf (21460/26740, elevation 468m (1536ft)).

From Barf take a good path westwards for 1km to Lord's Seat (20430/26560, elevation 552m (1811ft)) (2). (On the way we saw grouse amongst the heather.) To get the next objective, Ullister Hill, take the path south, to a stile over a fence. Go over the stile and follow a forest track to the left that swings towards Ullister Hill. At a post with a yellow marker, keep left and then 10m further on, leave the stony path for a muddy one on the right (20790/26280). This path goes to the mound at Ullister Hill (20940/26010, elevation 525m (1722ft)).

Walk to the mound and continue over it for a further 100m, on a thin path to another forest trail. Turn right, and then left at the next junction, by a post with a green marker (20810/25690). Then keep right and continue for 300m to a wide junction with a sign, Tarbarrel Moss (3). Turn right but immediately look for a path on the left, not signposted, just a few metres from the junction (20610/25440). Take this path through the trees to emerge onto open ground, over a stile in a corner. Follow the forest fence on the left for 500m until you are at the top of the ridge leading to Whinlatter. Take this ridge west, to the summit of Whinlatter Top (19700/24900, elevation 525m (1722ft)). There is another cairn and shelter further to the west at Brown How (19110/25140, elevation 517m (1696ft)) (4).

Return eastwards along the ridge to the edge of the forest. Descend steeply to a fence with a stile on the left; over which is a forest trail. This leads to a junction, by a seat. Turn right, downhill, in front of the seat and then, at a post with a green marker, turn left off the track. A path leads through the children's playground, to a metal sculpture of an osprey and the Visitors Centre. If you haven't been here before, the badger tunnel is a must, a highlight of the walk! The Centre has a shop, café, toilets and a small exhibition. At certain times of year, video cameras give live pictures of the osprey nest and a red squirrel site (5).

From the Centre take the track east, gradually downhill, past a cottage. At a junction the track bends left. Go a few steps further, then take a path on the right into the wood (21330/24980). Walk 50m, down to a stream. Continue east on this path and then cross a footbridge to the left bank. The path crosses a forest road and goes down to Comb Beck.

When we walked along here in January, we saw half a dozen, rather furtive-looking cavers. A tunnel, with a locked gate is on the left of the path (21940/25140). The cavers crossed the stream, climbed over a fence and disappeared from view, so I assume they used another mine entrance.

Continue on the path to Thornthwaite (6). In the village, opposite the cottages, look for a bear carved out of wood. Walk along a minor road, back to the car park at Powter How.

Although the Swan Inn has gone, the Royal Oak in Braithwaite has a good choice of Jennings' beers, including Cumberland Ale, Sneck Lifter and Cocker Hoop. Another good pub that closed quite a few years ago was the Horseshoe, on the other side of Whinlatter Pass in High Lorton. Its last night was particularly memorable!

# Walk 7. Eel Crag (Crag Hill) from Braithwaite

**Map:** OL4; map ref. prefix NY

**Distance:** 13.5km (8.5 miles)

**Ascent:** 1090m (3600ft)

**Time:** 6½ hours

**Starting point/parking:** In a small parking bay on the B5292 Whinlatter Pass, 500m from Braithwaite (227237).

## General Description

The path above Coledale Beck is taken to the head of the valley. The steep east face of Eel Crag (Crag Hill) is climbed using scree gullies and grass ledges (an alternative route is given). Sail and Causey Pike are visited. The way back is over Outerside and Barrow. Most of the route is on good paths. Force Crag mine is visited and there is aircraft wreckage on Eel Crag and Scar Crags.

## Route

At the end of the parking area go past the barrier and follow the track to the Force Crag mines. (From Braithwaite, walk up the Whinlatter Pass road and take the second path on the left, past a seat; this path joins the mine track.)

It is 4km (2.5 miles) along the track to Low Force Crag Mine (1). It was the route of the old mine tramway. On one walk I met two post-grads from Durham University who were researching the soil depth of the valley. They had expected a depth of 0.5m to 1.5m but their cross-sections across the valley had given a depth of up to 3m. Hammering probes to that depth looked like hard work.

Low Force Crag Mine closed in 1991 and was the last working mine in the Lakes. The buildings are still standing and there is a helpful information board provided by the National Trust. Tours around the inside of the buildings can be arranged. High Force and Low Force mines produced lead, zinc and barites (+ other 'ites' – there are specimens of sphalerite and cerusite, from these mines, in Manchester

Causey Pike

Museum). At High Force mine, the buildings are in poor condition, though one, by a tunnel with a warning notice, still has a fireplace. (Once, on the hillside between the mines, I disturbed a short-eared owl and I have seen grouse in this area.) Below the waterfalls by High Force Crag Mine, Pudding Beck drops down in another series of attractive falls, Low Force.

Continue past Low Force Mine on a faint path by the stream, to the left of the cliffs. At the top of the first rise, by a small dam, cross the main track and follow a beck south (195212) (2). Go through reeds and ascend the slope, past a sheepfold on the right, into the corrie below Eel Crag. The corrie looks as if it ought to contain a tarn as there is a good hollow for water to collect in, but no streams run down the surrounding slopes.

Walk south to the other side of the hollow where a sheepfold is hidden. On the way, a few pieces of wreckage may be spotted, from a Halifax bomber that crashed in January 1944. The aircraft was being

The view from Causey Pike

ferried from Kinloss to Wiltshire. The two aircrew were killed. More wreckage has been placed in the sheepfold (19545/20525) (3). The plane crashed into the face of Eel Crag just below the summit. The trail of wreckage lies all the way down the face and may be followed, past the impact site, to the summit, (The next paragraph describes an alternative route.) Return to the west of the hollow, to the bottom of the scree and make your way up it, looking for wreckage. As the slope steepens, the trail tends to the left. At the top of the scree, climb up one of the gullies to the left of the main face. A relatively safe route to the top can be found, using grass ledges. The highest point of the wreckage, a small piece of molten metal, was 100 feet below the summit (19358/20369). The elevation given by my GPS was 810m. At the end of the route description there are more map references of the wreckage. From here, ascend directly up to a stone shelter at the top of Eel Crag. The summit cairn lies 50m away (19260/20360, elevation 839m (2752ft)) (4).

If you wish to avoid this rather steep route and the scree, an alter-

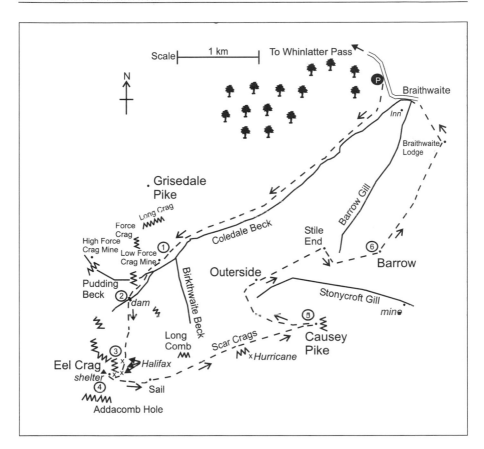

native way to the summit from the bottom of the crags, is to climb diagonally to the right (NW) to gain the north ridge of Eel Crag. Follow a grassy slope that goes through a gap in the crags, (19290/20750), aiming for a flat section of the ridge.

(I once saw seven kestrels quartering the west side of Eel Crag. To the south is the impressive, deep cove of Addacomb Hole.)

From the cairn on Eel Crag, the path to Sail starts in a SE direction and swings to the east above the crags. Continue to Sail, the distance from Eel Crag is 600m. The path passes just to the south of the summit (19800/20280, elevation 773m (2536ft)). Keep on the easterly path for another 1km to Scar Crags.

In 1941 a Hurricane, a fighter aircraft, crashed into the crags below, to the south. Very small fragments of wreckage lie in a narrow gully below a point on the ridge (21008/20755). I found wreckage in the scree about 40m down at around 2000ft (21023/20691 & 21008/20755). There are more pieces below. Rich Allenby's website gives information about aircraft wreck sites, see appendix. His wife, Caroline, discovered the wreckage; she must have excellent eyesight and nimble feet! Continue along the ridge, over four small bumps to Causey Pike (21870/20850, elevation 637m (2090ft)) (5). From the cairn there are excellent views over Derwent Water.

Double back along the path to Sail for 300m, and take a path to the right, not marked on the map (21550/20880). It leads, on a bearing of 300°, to a mine track to the south of Outerside.

This track, which goes towards Sail Pass from Stonycroft, was constructed in 1855 by the Keswick Mining Company in a search for cobalt. Some was mined near Long Comb but the venture failed. Further down the track, below Barrow, were ore smelters. Glazed slag may be seen in rubble, below a clearing not far from the road. In an early disaster, a dam in the gill burst killing several miners. A lead mine tunnel is next to Stonycroft Gill. Stonechats may be seen lower down the valleys in this area.

Cross the mine track and walk to the top of Outerside (21100/21460). Follow the path off Outerside, bearing of 060°, to Stile End. Continue eastwards over Barrow (6) and descend NE along the ridge to Braithwaite. Again, there are fine views of Derwent Water and of Skiddaw beyond Braithwaite.

The public bar of the Coledale Inn, on the west side of the village, has a good selection of ales.

### *Note:*

Map refs. of the Halifax wreckage found below Eel Crag: 19501/20653, 19380/20578, 19344/20598, 19337/20439, 19367/20401, 19361/20389.

# Walk 8. Skiddaw from Bassenthwaite

**Map:** OL4; map ref. prefix NY

**Distance:** 15km (9.5 miles)

**Ascent:** 970m (3200ft)

**Time:** 6½ hours

**Starting point/parking:** In Bassenthwaite: by the triangular green (229321) or by Halls Beck (230323). Alternatively, there are spaces for several cars where the route crosses a minor road near Peter House Farm (249323). (This slightly alters the start and finish of the walk.)

## General Description

The route climbs Skiddaw by the side of a quiet gill. From the summit the pleasant, quite popular way over Carl Side and Ullock Pike is followed. Most of the walk is on good paths. The advantage of starting in Bassenthwaite is the visit to a lovely village and the Sun Inn at the finish.

## Route

From Bassenthwaite take the track, signposted to Peter House Farm, by the bus stop at the eastern corner of the triangular green. Walk for 200m and take the left fork heading eastwards. After two fields the path crosses to the right-hand edge of the field. Continue along the fence, through gates or stiles to the road near Peter House Farm (1). (This is the alternative starting point/parking.)

Cross the road and take a good track towards Whitewater Dash Waterfall. Notice the strange lump of Brockle Crag to the north. After a further 1.5km, Dead Beck and the beginning of open-access land are reached (2). The route goes up by the side of Dead Beck but to get a better view of Dash Falls, make a short trip along the track and, after seeing the falls, return to Dead Beck. One could continue past the Dash Falls and ascend the path to Bakestall, but the way by Dead Beck is more interesting. Climb steeply on the west side of the beck. When I was there in September, the cascades were very attractive and, except

SKIDDAW        CARL        ULLOCK
               SIDE        PIKE

Skiddaw from near Bassenthwaite

for a couple of places, it is possible to stay by the water most of the way. A mossy waterfall, by a fallen tree, is bypassed on the right.

Higher up, the beck enters a narrow gorge. Close to the water, on the west side, is the dripping, mossy entrance of an old lead mine (262311). Continue by the beck until it enters a boggy area then go SW to gain the wide ridge of Broad End. (Low down, a pair of kestrels were hovering over the fell, whilst higher, several ravens were riding the thermals.) Climb the gentle slope to meet the path by the fence that comes up from Bakestall. Here, I met a group of women descending from Skiddaw. One of them had the bright idea of using a hair band as a temporary repair to a flapping boot sole. 1km further south is Skiddaw's summit with a trig point and direction indicator (26040/29090, elevation (931m (3053ft)) (3). The small wood surrounding Skiddaw House may be seen in the distance, to the east.

From the summit go south, past several cairns, to the southern end of the ridge. One winter, along here, a ferocious wind forced Jan and I

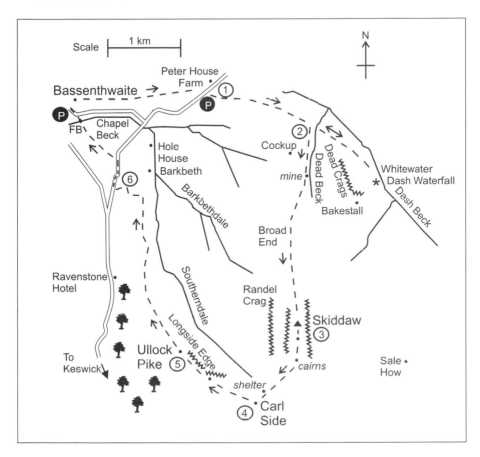

to crawl on our hands and knees in the snow. My hat was torn off and disappeared towards Blencathra; conditions were so bad that we turned back 200m short of the summit. Take the path that descends steeply SW, on scree, towards Carl Side (260286). A good spot for a rest and refreshments is a small shelter, with views down Southerndale, 50m NE of Carlside Tarn.

From the tarn, go 200m SW to the top of Carl Side (25480/28090, elevation 746m (2447ft)) (4). Walk on a bearing of 300° to Longside Edge which leads to Ullock Pike (24450/28730, elevation 692m (2270ft)) (5). The path continues northwards for over 2km, with fine views of Bassenthwaite. At the end of the ridge a wall is reached. Climb a stile and go north, past a standing stone, to a gate on the left,

Carlside Tarn

near the end of the field. The path bends down to a minor road (6). This is the one crossed much earlier and leads to the parking area by Peter House Farm.

Turn right along the road for 450m. Go over a stile on the left and walk, 150m NW, to a footbridge. Over this, turn left along the edge of the field. This leads to a stile in a corner; cross this and follow the fence as it bends left. Walk towards a wood, with a hedge on your right. Over a stile, the path leads to a footbridge. On the other side, go straight ahead to a lane and walk back to the village.

The Sun Inn is a Jennings pub with a selection of ales including Fish King. This is named after the ospreys that breed in woods on the west side of Bassenthwaite. The RSPB have telescopes set up in the breeding season in Dodd Wood, near Mirehouse; these are for public use and are free.

# Walk 9. Blencathra and Great Calva from Threlkeld

**Maps:** OL4 & OL5; map ref. prefix NY

**Distance:** 17km (10.5 miles)

**Ascent:** 1130m (3700ft)

**Time:** 7½ hours

**Starting point/parking:** Off the A66 in Threlkeld. Turn right, up a cul-de-sac, towards the Blencathra Centre. The car park is 400m along the road (318256).

## General Description

The start of the climb up Blencathra is alongside Blease Gill. The path on Gategill Fell is joined and followed to the summit ridge. From Blencathra the walk goes down to the River Caldew. It continues up Great Calva and then down to Skiddaw House. The return is along Glenderaterra Beck. About half this walk is off-path. Some boggy, tussocky and heathery terrain is met. A mining area, a fine sheepfold and a tiny bothy are visited. I chose a lovely, sunny March day when the top of Blencathra was covered in snow.

## Route

Take the path, sign-posted Blencathra, north from the car park for 400m along the side of a beck. Go through a gate, cross the path that runs to the south of Blencathra, and continue north by the side of Blease Gill. After a series of small, mossy waterfalls you are forced away from the gill. I started on the left bank then soon switched to the right side, keeping as close as possible to the water. The going gets easier higher up. Where the gill forks, go to the right (31510/26700) (1). The water flows through a narrow ravine and it is possible to scramble along the rocky bed, though I did have difficulty on icy patches. After 200m the ravine opens out and the beck flows through a 30m wide gulch. Continue up the scree but higher up, as it becomes looser, escape to the grass at the right edge. Eventually, the path along the ridge of Gategill Fell is reached (31840/27280). The ridge leads steeply to the main path along the top of the cliffs. I had a small

Blencathra from St John's in the Vale

cornice to break through at the top. Blencathra's summit cairn is 500m to the NE (32340/27730, elevation 868m (2847ft)) (2).

From the summit go north for 200m to a cross, made from white, quartz rocks. This is 40m south of the small tarn that lies in the saddle. Continue north, past a cairn to another, larger cross, also made from quartz rocks, 200m south of the cairn on Atkinson Pike. This memorial was originally smaller but was extended over a period of time by a Mr Robinson. Go to Atkinson Pike and walk NW down a path, over scree. At the bottom, take a path, bearing of 300°, across Mungrisdale Common; frozen when I was there in March but usually boggy. After just over 1km, a cairn is reached (31050/29230) (3).

Continue on a bearing of 300°, off-path, dropping down to the River Caldew and aiming for a circular sheepfold on the far side. The going is easy until you get close to the river, where it becomes tussocky and boggy. Cross the River Caldew; this may involve getting your feet wet, but I was lucky and found some rocks. I congratulated

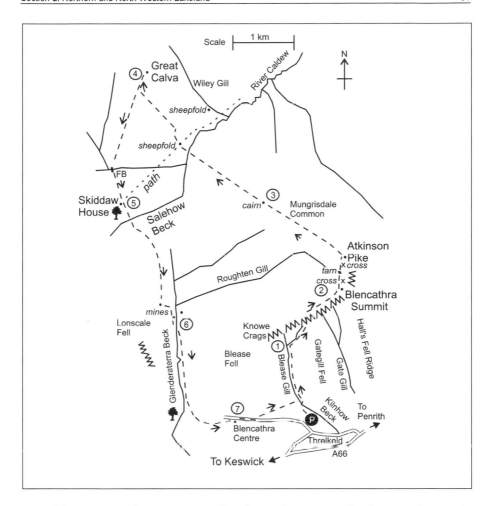

myself too soon because on the far side, my right leg sunk up to mid-thigh in a very cold sump of muddy water. Go to the sheepfold to inspect its fine construction (29660/30120).

The next target is Great Calva, though it could be omitted from the day's agenda and the path along the river taken directly to Skiddaw House. It is a steep flog, over awkward ground, to Great Calva but if it is clear the views from the top will repay the effort. Start on a sheep track that slants right from the sheepfold to a grassy gap in the heather; this is a good way to gain height. Higher up the heather gets shorter and easier. An old grouse butt may be seen (29350/30360),

Blencathra summit

with another, 40m further on. I did see a grouse near here and also a stonechat. Aim NW, to the left of the summit where a good path is met coming up from the direction of Skiddaw House. This leads, past the obligatory false summit (with an iron bar protruding from it), to the cairn at the true summit (29080/31180, elevation 690m (2265ft)) (4). Criffel, in Scotland, may be seen across the Solway Firth.

An energetic soul might continue to Little Calva but the path down to Skiddaw House is tempting. This returns past the false summit and is a pleasant way to lose height. It meets the main valley path, 200m north of a footbridge (28400/29840). Follow this path southwards to Skiddaw House. There is a small bothy, 3m by 2m, providing emergency shelter, at the north end of the building. At the south side of the building are two picnic tables, an obvious place for a rest and refreshment. Skiddaw House was originally built as a shooting lodge. Used by shepherds until the last one retired, it is now a Youth Hostel (5).

From Skiddaw House continue SE, then south for 1.5km until the path forks. The right fork goes south round the side of Lonscale Fell in the direction of Keswick. The left one heads over Glenderaterra Beck, beneath Blease Fell, to Threlkeld. (I was interested in the spoil heap just below the Lonscale Fell path so I continued along that for 400m and dropped down to inspect it. There isn't much there, apart from a collapsed mine entrance (29340/27550).)

Take the left fork down to Glenderaterra Beck, leave the path and follow the beck south, to an old copper mine (6). The workings are interesting and the way along the beck is enjoyable. There is a mine entrance with a wet floor by the beck (29680/27370), ruined buildings, bits of pipe and other fragments that might mean something to an expert.

A track leads away from the mine and crosses the beck. Follow this for over 1km, as it heads south past a wood. Go through a gate and over a stile on the left (29935/25460). Walk 80m up a slope to a gate into a wood (I saw a flock of long-tailed tits here). Follow the path up, through the wood to the Blencathra Centre (7). Signs direct you through a farm to a road that leads back to the car park. Along the road, take a path signed 'PERMISSIVE FOOTPATH TO BLEASE GILL'. This leads, through fields, back to the top of the wood by Blease Gill. Turn right, the walk along the beck makes a nice finish. (Near here, I saw a pair of crows mob a buzzard and later, another buzzard flew close by and landed on a wall.)

There are two good pubs in Threlkeld, The Salutation and The Horse and Farrier.

### Note:

The mine at Gate Gill, and the nearby Woodend mine, produced large quantities of galena and zinc.

# *Walk 10. A Newlands Round*

**Map:** OL4; map ref. prefix NY

**Distance:** 18km (11 miles)

**Ascent:** 1300m (4270ft)

**Time:** 8 hours

**Starting point/parking:** Space for several cars by a sharp bend on the New-lands valley road, on the north side of bridge over Rigg Beck 4km from Braithwaite, on the way to Newlands Hause (229201).

## General description

The start is along the Newlands Valley. The route goes over Dale Head, Hindscarth and Robinson. The return is by Knott Rigg and Ard Crags. The route is mainly on good paths but short sections are over boggy or tussocky ground. Features include several old copper mines, a waterfall, an old church and an unusual ravine.

## Route

From the car park (an old quarry area), walk 100m eastwards along the road, then turn sharp right and go across a footbridge. (The Mill Dam Inn once stood by the beck.) Walk south along the road for 600m until close to Chapel Bridge. Turn right, signposted Newlands Church and turn left opposite the church, where there is a plaque with information about the old school room. Inside, there is further information and a Wordsworth poem mentioning the church.

Walk to Low Snab Farm and go through a gate on the far side. Spoil heaps from the Goldscope Mine, first worked for copper in the early part of the 13th century, are on the hillside to the right. A climb above a spoil heap reveals a tunnel (228185). There are more worked out rakes above but only the lower level warrants a visit. The mine was a key producer of copper and lead but silver and gold were also extracted. It has a very deep shaft; working stopped due to flooding. English Heritage lists it as a major national site. Drop down to the bottom of the valley and cross the footbridge (1). Continue south, past the Carlisle Mountaineering Club Hut, for 1.5km to Castlenook Mine.

Newlands Church

There is little to see of the old copper mine. Keep on the path to the east side of the beck for a further 800m, past Far Tongue Gill to a sheepfold. On the west bank there is an open level (22850/16270). There are further gashes in the ground above here, Long Work openworks, where mining has taken place. Above is a waterfall, by the path to Dalehead Tarn. Go west for 300m, to another sheepfold and more mine workings by Far Tongue Gill.

Now, either follow Far Tongue Gill uphill or, to visit another open mine level climb to a spoil heap 300m further to the west. The tunnel has a low entrance but then opens out (22460/16210). Take the miners' path that climbs diagonally from here to Far Tongue Gill.

This path continues past the gill, but the ravine formed by the gill makes a more interesting route (2). (The path is rejoined later with a little loss of height). The ascent of the 800m long ravine is easy. A small stream flows down over a variety of rocks and there are one or two water features. Near the end of the ravine, escape up the bank to

Dale Head Summit

the left (21880/15910). Turn back, to the left, and aim to rejoin the mine path. Contour round the side of a large hollow, across scree, to a ruined mine building (22200/15680).

The miners' path is well defined and climbs steadily. At one point a sheep track goes straight on but the path turns right, up the hillside (22240/15630). This leads to Dalehead Mine. The level is filled in, but many of the stones show the green streaks of malachite. The path continues above Great Gable (Gable Crag) to join the main path from Dalehead Tarn (22550/15500). If you drop down a few steps you may see the tarn. Climb to the finely constructed cairn at the summit of Dale Head (22330/15330, elevation 753m (2472ft)) (3).

Continue westwards along the path and, after 1km, take the path that branches right to Hindscarth (21500/15746). Far Tongue Gill may be seen below, to the east, from the edge of the ridge. Hindscarth summit has a shelter (21560/16510, elevation 727m (2385ft)). There is another, well-built shelter 200m to the north.

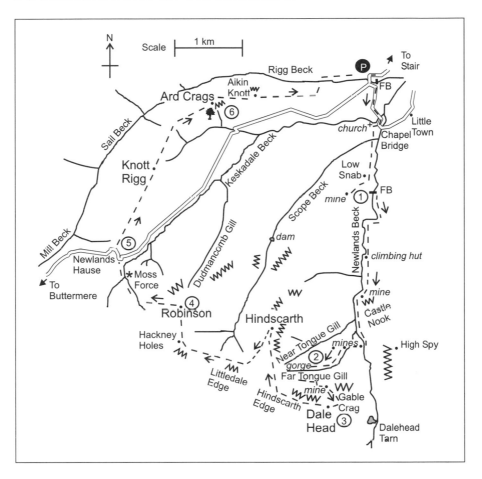

Leave the summit on a path, a few metres to the west of the one you arrived on. The path isn't immediately clear but it is soon picked up. (Along here, a small pool contained tadpoles.) The path slants across to the fence and along Littledale Edge (20760/16100). Drop down to the col below Robinson and then climb uphill by the fence. Just before the top of the slope, step over the fence to inspect a large, deep gash in the ground, named Hackney Holes (20240/16310). The rocks near the top have many quartz veins and there are good views of Buttermere below. Go north to the summit of Robinson (20180/16869, elevation 737m (2418ft)) (4).

Aim west from the cairn, off-path, dropping down the grassy slope, past small crags. Swing NW over tussocky and boggy ground, aiming for the top of Moss Force. Cross to the other side of Moss Beck. There is a path further to the west that descends to Newlands Hause, but it is possible to climb down close to the waterfall without too much difficulty. To do this, at the top of the fall, on the west side and next to the water, step down onto mossy, wet ground. Work your way down grass ledges on the left and then descend over loose stones to the main waterfall path. It is easy to see why it is called Moss Force. Walk down to the car parks by the road at Newlands Hause (elevation 333m, (1093ft)) (5).

Go across the road to a path leading up to Knott Rigg. There were many bags of stone lying by the path, indicating that it was about to be repaired. There is a small cairn at Knott Rigg summit (19740/18870, elevation 556m (1824ft)).

Continue along the ridge to Ard Crags where there are fine, all-round views (20688/19770, elevation 581m (1906ft)) (6). Drop steeply down from Aikin Knott and, where the slope starts to ease, look for a path that branches left (21890/19920). It slants down diagonally to Rigg Beck and joins the main valley path above the far bank. From here, the car park is less than 1km away.

Just round the corner from the car park is/was a remarkable purple, wooden house. It has been a landmark for decades but has fallen into decay. The last time I saw it there was a demolition sign outside. Apparently, a Canadian had it built in the late 19th century. At one time it was a lodging house for actors, including Tom Courtenay, who appeared at the theatre in Keswick. Ted Hughes, the poet, often stayed there.

If you go through nearby Stair, notice a cottage with the year 1647, the letters FF and a cross, carved in stone above the doorway.

The Mill Dam Inn would have been very handy but the Swinside Inn, 2km away on the road through Stair, is a very attractive old inn, serving Theakston's and Jennings.

# Walk 11. Knott and High Pike from Caldbeck

**Maps:** OL4 & OL5; map ref. prefix NY

**Distance:** 27km (17 miles)

**Ascent:** 970m (3200ft)

**Time:** 10½ hours

**Starting point/parking:** Free car park in Caldbeck, just north of the bridge over the river (323399).

## General Description

The walk starts along Whelpo Beck, goes through fields to Fell Side and on to Roughton Gill. This gives the possibility of an easy scramble. Great Sca Fell, Knott, Carrock Fell and High Pike are visited. Much of the walk is on good paths, though some of it is over awkward, tussocky terrain. Several mines and an Iron-Age Fort are visited. Among the birds that may be seen are dippers, curlews, wheatears, grouse, buzzards and skylarks.

## Route

Leave the car park at the west side and walk along a road that goes north and bends round houses, back to the beck. There is a sign indicating ¼ mile to The Howk. The route goes right, past a garden to a path along the north bank of Whelpo Beck and leads to the ruins of a bobbin mill (319397). The mill ran from 1857-1924 and employed 60 men and boys. There are steps 30m past the mill. On the other side of the railings are rocks and the adventurous may scramble through a hole between them. The rock is limestone and the walk along the gorge, the Howk, makes a pleasant start to the day. You may see dippers here, flying above the water. Continue west along the river to a road bridge 1.5km from the car park.

Cross the bridge and turn right along the road for 100m to Whelpo Farm (1). Take a sign-posted path, on the left, past farm buildings. This goes through fields to a minor road. Here, turn left and after 200m, right, along a road that leads to Fell Side. (There were curlews

Bobbin Mill, The Howk

in the fields making their liquid calls.) Go past the outdoor centre and turn left up a wide track. Continue to a gate and turn right where the mine road to Roughton Gill is signposted. Take this to the side of Dale Beck. On the left is Hay Gill, which, if you have time to explore, is an attractive beck (301361). It has a mine tunnel 100m away (302361), and another, with water flowing out, further on.

Back at Dale Beck, follow the main mine track all the way to a hut at the bottom of the waterfalls of Roughton Gill (2). Behind the hut is a shaft with a locked metal cover. The main ore mined in this area was lead but some copper was also extracted. Start up the left side of the gill on loose spoil. About 200m up the gill, on the left by an 8ft waterfall, is a tunnel (30220/34260). By torchlight (from the entrance!) it looked in good condition. Scramble up the stream to two more tunnels. The one on the right is called a coffin level because it is wider at shoulder height and narrower lower down (the cross-section is coffin-shaped) (30200/34240). My comrade explored a few steps inside and said that it split into two but that neither branch went far. Whilst cowering by the entrance, I found a small stone-axe. It is in

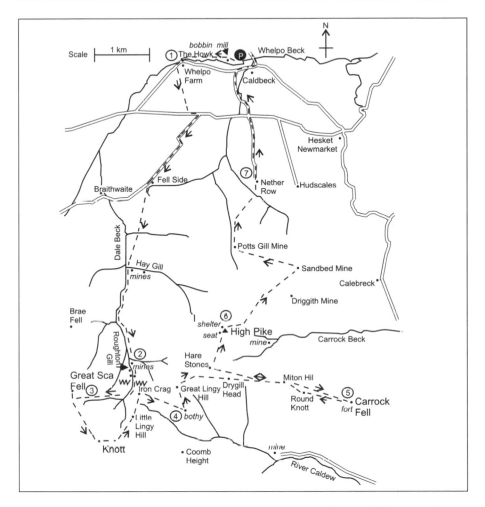

excellent condition, with a polished finish and it still has a sharp edge. This could be evidence that the seam was worked thousands of years ago when the ore would have shown as an outcrop on the surface, or the axe could have got there by some other means. Near here, on the left by a 15ft waterfall, is another tunnel entrance, behind a large boulder.

Continue to scramble up, or by the side of, the gill. It is a very pretty stream and the scrambling is relatively easy. At the top of the gill there is a waterfall with a 15ft rock wall on its right. I climbed

The top of Roughton Gill

nearly to the top of this only to slide back down when my foothold gave way.

The gill splits into three by the ruined walls of a shelter. 30m up the middle branch are the signs of a mine. Rocks form retaining walls but the hillside has collapsed over the entrance. In front of the ruins take the right branch of the gill (30010/33790). Follow this, westwards for 800m until it peters out. Walk 400m northwards to Great Sca Fell (29130/33890, elevation 651m (2136ft)) (3). Return south to the saddle below Knott and take the path that rises SE to Knott (29620/32980, elevation 710m (2329ft)).

From Knott go east for about 400m, then swing NE over boggy ground aiming for a slightly raised hump, by Miller Moss, named Little Lingy Hill (30180/33380).

Go north to a cairn above Iron Crag (30360/33890). From here, head 120° to an old shooting cabin that is now a small bothy (31170/33580) (4). Go past small pools of water, trying to keep on the same contour line. The hut is hidden until the last few steps. Here, at Lingy Hut, we met a man who explained that a book used to be kept, in which visitors wrote their names, this included some Russians who had been there recently. Sadly it had disappeared and it's difficult to imagine why someone should remove a worthless object that gave a little pleasure to fellow walkers.

From the hut, a path heads north towards Great Lingy Hill (31010/33970, elevation 616m (2021ft)). To the SE of Great Lingy Hill is Carrock Mine, by Grainsgill Beck. Initially this area was mined for lead, later wolfram, from which tungsten is produced, was extracted. It was last worked in 1981 and was the only mine in the country to produce wolfram.

If you have the time, take a trip to Carrock Fell, just over 3km from Great Lingy Hill, along a long, but easy ridge. Go NE for 200m, then contour round to meet the path over Miton Hill. There is a small pike, with a cairn, named Round Knott; I bypassed it on the way there and visited it on the way back (33430/33720). Carrock Fell is the site of an ancient hill fort and it is still possible to see the position of the walls. The highest point is to the west (34170/33630, elevation 663m (2174ft)) (5). 2km to the south, across the valley, the secretive Bowscale Tarn may be seen.

Return west along the path, to the col between Great Lingy Hill and High Pike. The path swings north and rises gently to High Pike. There is a trig point and a stone bench at the summit (31870/35000, elevation 658m (2159ft)) (6). The bench replaces an earlier one and commemorates Mick Lewis and Millicent Mary Lewis of Badger Hill, Nether Row. An inscription says:

> "He is a portion of that loveliness that once he made more lovely"

100m to the north, is a stone shelter. From here, drop NE to a path above Driggith Mine. Initially this produced copper and lead, and then later, barytes. A deep shaft is fenced off and a trench runs for several hundred metres. Stay on the main path for 700m (32680/35800). Then drop down the slope, eastwards, to Sandbed Mine, past four fenced-off areas, one of the lower ones contains a flooded shaft. There are spoil heaps and trenches amongst the evidence of earlier mining activities (330360). A wide mine track starts to the NW, rising slightly as it curves round the hillside. Take this for just over 1km to Potts Gill Mine (320367). Again, there are numerous fenced-off shafts and spoil heaps. From here, take a good track north towards Nether Row (7). 200m down the hill, a grassy path on the left cuts off a few metres; it passes a large boulder. Go past Clay Bottom Farm, where I saw an attractive owl design in a window. Continue north to Caldbeck.

The Oddfellows Arms is well placed and the Jennings Bitter very refreshing.

*Opposite: Fat Man's Agony (Walk 14)*

# Section 3: Southern Lakeland

# Walk 12. Broad Crag and the Scafells from Wasdale Head

**Map:** OL6; map ref. prefix NY

**Distance:** 12.5km (8 miles)

**Ascent:** 1360m (4500ft)

**Time:** 7½ hours

**Starting point/parking:** Wasdale Village Green, 1km north of Wast Water (186085). (There is a plaque, worth reading, on a rock at the entrance to the Green.)

## General Description

The route goes to Piers Gill, Broad Crag and on to Scafell Pike. Then it drops down towards Eskdale. The climb up to Scafell is by the side of How Beck (no path). There is a choice between a straightforward path down from Scafell or a more adventurous way by Deep Ghyll and Lord's Rake. There are some good paths with a little easy scrambling. Two aircraft crash sites may be visited.

## Route

Walk up the track from the NE corner of Wasdale Village Green to Wasdale Church. Go inside and read the small inscription in a small windowpane. Also, look at the headstones of climbers' graves in the NW corner of the graveyard. Continue past Burnthwaite, on the path leading to Sty Head. Where the path gets close to Lingmell Beck, leave it and follow the beck (201092). Near a rowan tree and pool, cross the beck and as soon as possible use the stream bed. There is a nice water slide by a holly tree. The next bit looks tricky but a long step on the right wall enables you to follow the water. Take the right fork (212092). After 500m, at the next fork, go right to Piers Gill (214087) (1). In July 1921 a Mr Crump fell in Piers Gill and survived 20 days before being found.

After 100m the gill enters a ravine. This is a good place to exit, to a path on the left. If you wish to sample the atmosphere of Piers Gill continue for a further 50m or so and then escape up a grassy slope on

Mosedale from near Scafell Pike

the left, by a small gully. This leads to a rock wall that is bypassed on the left and the path along the top of the gill is gained. It leads to a short rock face that provides an easy scramble, indicated by an arrow scratched on a rock (21290/08300). Continue to the top of Piers Gill.

Immediately above here, to the SE are crags that give a short scramble. From the left of centre, use ledges to climb to the top. Walk along the top and cross a path by a cairn (215077). The buttress ahead provides excellent holds and gives a fine route all the way to the summit of Broad Crag. It can be as easy as you wish to make it. There is the option, on the way, of diverting left to the site of an aircraft wreck. In 1946 a De Havilland Dominie, an air ambulance, crashed into Broad Crag killing the patient and four crew. The wreckage includes the two engines (21720/07755 and 21770/07805) (2). After visiting the crash site, angle back to the right, to continue the scramble up the best rock (21680/07640). There doesn't appear to be a cairn at the summit of Broad Crag (21860/07560, elevation 931m (3054ft)).

Go SE to join the M1 to Scafell Pike (21540/07230, elevation 978m (3210ft)) (3). Apart from the raised platform, there is a trig point and

SCAFELL PIKE

ROUGH CRAG

Cross on Scafell

several shelters. The best shelter is 50m away, bearing 060°. Some of you may be happy to return to Wasdale at this point but I suggest you continue to Scafell by the following route.

Leave Scafell Pike SW and make your way for 400m through a boulder field to visit the highest tarn in the Lakes, Broadcrag Tarn (21310/06920, elevation 837m (2746ft), depth 3ft). En route, you pass through a stone-axe factory area. I have found a stone that is partially chipped (though this might have been due to natural weathering). From the tarn head south, taking care to find a safe way past sloping rock plates. Opposite, is the climbing area of Scafell East Buttress. Join the path heading down towards Eskdale. The path to Foxes Tarn is one possibility, but my route goes lower and climbs up to Scafell by the side of How Beck. Leave the path (21400/06140) and contour SW, below crags, to How Beck. Follow this as it rises, into a fine, remote corrie.

In 1943 a trainer aircraft, an Anson, crashed near the top of the ridge. I found wreckage, some of it painted yellow, in many places. Pieces of wreckage are near a cairn on a boulder at the entrance to the corrie (20975/05914). Ascend the scree on the right, passing pieces of wreckage, to the point of impact of the aircraft at the top of the slope

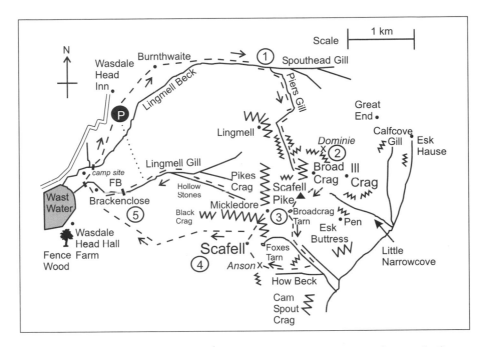

(20845/06170). This is less than 20m from a cairn on the path from Slight Side to Scafell. Join this path and turn right. (Tragically, if the aircraft had been flying only a few feet higher it might not have crashed.) Walk 400m to the summit cairn of Scafell (20680/06480, elevation 964m (3162ft)) (4). More map references of wreckage are listed after this description.

Continue northwards for 150m along a path, past a shelter. On the ground is a large cross, made from stones. There is the option of an easy way down to Wasdale or the more adventurous route of the West Wall Traverse and Lord's Rake. The easy path descends west from a cairn (20720/06610). It continues steadily down towards Fence Wood above Wasdale Head Farm, past Brackenclose, to the car park at Wasdale Village Green.

Lord's Rake is an interesting way to descend from Scafell, but a few years ago a large boulder became detached and is now perched dangerously at the top. Going down Lord's Rake from the top would involve passing the boulder but this can be avoided by going down Deep Ghyll and along the West Wall Traverse to enter Lord's Rake just below the boulder. This does not eliminate the risk, as one day it will leave its perch and wipe out everything below. I will describe the route but you have been warned. From the stone cross, 150m from the summit of Scafell, continue northwards (030°) to the top of Deep Ghyll. (On the way a short visit to the peak on the left gives a fine view of Scafell Pinnacle.) The start of Deep Ghyll is marked by a cairn (20820/06717). The stones at the top of the gill are reddish and very loose. Drop steeply, and carefully, into the gill from the right side. Go down the loose stones for 50m until the gully steepens. The surrounding walls are historic climbing areas and this enclosed space has a daunting atmosphere. Look for a path on the left, the West Wall Traverse; it is essential that you don't miss it. It is not difficult and leads into Lord's Rake where the detached boulder can be seen, all too well!

Tiptoe right, down loose scree, it isn't quite as bad as it looks. At the bottom look for a faint cross, etched in the wall at head height, just before the path ahead rises, along Rake's Progress (20770/06880). It is a memorial to four climbers killed in 1903. On my recent visit I couldn't see the cross at first because it has become faded. Two climbers, Graham and Mike looked in their guidebook for information to help me. I'd seen them earlier, climbing on the east buttress of Scafell. They'd been on routes that must have been greasy in the cloudy conditions. I think they had been climbing *Great Eastern* when I saw them.

From the memorial the route goes left, west, down scree, to join the main path through Hollow Stones and Brown Tongue. There is a short cut to the car park (19010/07350). If you continue down Lingmell Gill, go over a footbridge to a wood. The low building in the trees is Brackenclose, the headquarters of the Fell and Rock Climbing Club (5).

The Wasdale Head Inn is steeped in the history of climbing and has many old photographs. Also, it serves a good selection of beers.

### Note:

Wreckage map references: 21323/05972 (10m left of where water flows steeply down mossy steps); 21140/05933; 21030/05952; 20990/05944; 20975/05914 (near a boulder with a cairn on top); 20951/05926 (following scree to the right); 20923/06093; 20915/06173; 20911/06134; 20900/06168; 20896/06194; 20862/06163; and several pieces near the top of the ridge, close to the impact site (20845/06170).

# Walk 13. Coniston Old Man and Brim Fell from Coniston

**Map:** OL6

**Distance:** 13.5km (8.5 miles)

**Ascent:** 1000m (3280ft)

**Time:** 6½ hours

**Starting point/parking:** Take the road to the south of Church Beck that climbs past the Sun Hotel and leads to Walna Scar Road. There is a large car park at the end of the road (SD 288969). Water often runs across this road and in winter this can form black ice. In such conditions it is safer to park a few hundred metres before the car park or lower down in Coniston.

## General Description

The route goes to Levers Water and follows Cove Beck to the summit of Brim Fell.

Coniston Old Man is visited and then the ridge is followed to Swirl How. The descent is by the Prison Band and back to Levers Water. Some of the walk is on paths but Gill Cove is pathless. The direct way up Brim Fell is steep though it is possible to avoid this. There is a possibility of some short scrambles. The crash sites of two aircraft are visited and the whole area is littered with evidence of copper mining. When I did this walk in December the paths were very icy and the higher ground was frozen.

## Route

From the car park, take the track that leaves on the north side. After 500m there is the option of an easy scramble up The Bell (Grade 1). This is the little peak, 300m to the right of the path. There is an obvious rib that leads up its southern side. It's as easy as you want to make it and is a good warm up for the day (1). To get to it, leave the track and take a path, close to a wall, through bracken. After The Bell go NW, cross a path heading to Coniston Old Man (SD 28420/98083), and take the path northwards to a bridge over Low Water Beck by a large boulder, the Pudding Stone. For some sport, scramble to the top of this; a

The view from Coniston Old Man

friend, Brian once fell off and landed on a convenient flat rock at the base.

A spoil heap is visible, to the west, below Brim Fell and there is a tunnel above it, the Brim Fell Level (SD 27850/98480). It is over 50m long with a masonry roof for the first 15m. A friend has explored it and says that it is safe to enter!

Over the bridge by the Pudding Stone, take a path, NE, below Grey Crag to Levers Water Beck (2). Recently, I met two shepherds here with five dogs, rounding up sheep, "that time of year" one of them said. Over the next hour or so they covered the fells above and around Levers Water, at an impressive speed.

There are tunnels, part of the Paddy End Copper Works, on the far side of the footbridge over the Levers Water Beck, one close by the beck, called Hospital Level, and another, 30m further on, called Courteney's Cross Cut. These are dangerous and shouldn't be explored beyond the entrances. If there isn't too much water, Levers

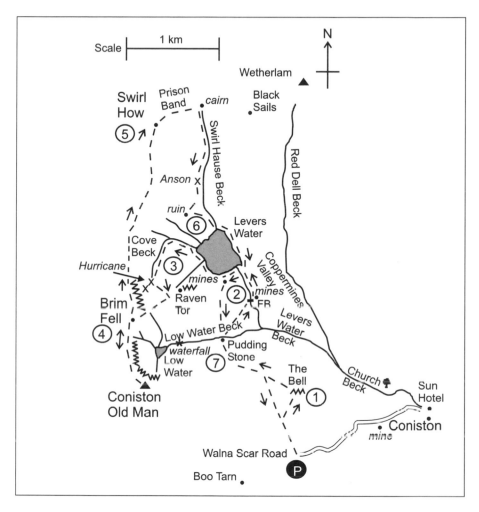

Water Beck is a pleasant, Grade 1 scramble. There is more evidence of mining activities by the beck, including an incline to the left of the footbridge. There had been heavy rain the last time I visited, so I took the path up the left side. In such conditions the waterfalls are very impressive.

From the reservoir dam, take the path round the west side of Levers Water. At the westernmost tip, Cove Beck flows into the reservoir (SD 276993). Leave the path and follow this as it curves south, round crags, into Gill Cove (3). Follow Cove Beck as goes up a lovely valley. High up on the right is the main ridge leading to Coniston Old Man. At the end of the beck there is a scree slope on the right that leads steeply to the top of Brim Fell. Amongst the scree are fragments from a fighter aircraft, a Hurricane. This was one of two that crashed here in 1943; tragically both pilots were killed. The lowest pieces I found are at SD 27239/98975, elevation 650m. The highest fragments are 60m below the summit, just below a vertical crag (SD 27139/98873, elevation 740m). When we were there the ground was frozen, with an icy glaze on the rocks and in such conditions I would not advise climbing directly up here.

To avoid the steep slope, go SE from the top of the Cove Beck onto Brim Fell Rake. Aim for the saddle by Raven Tor ( SD 27510/98800). Then go west to the summit of Brim Fell (SD 27060/98550, elevation 796m (2611ft)) (4).

Walk south for 1km to the top of The Old Man (SD 27220/97820, elevation 803m (2633ft)). To the west arc views of the climbing area of Dow Crag and, to the SW, look for Blind Tarn, hidden below Brown Pike. If you want a short day, one way off the top is to go south from the cairn on a pleasant path, past quarries, swinging SE down to Boo Tarn. An alternative exploration is to the quarries on the SW flank of Coniston Old Man. Care is needed to find a way past the vertical walls. The workings are extensive. A tunnel goes in a short way with some pieces of rail and sleepers inside (SD 27170/97250). An old mining hut has been taken over by a climbing club (SD 27090/97060). It is called the Jack Diamond Memorial Climbing Hut. He was a member of the Coniston Tigers, along with A. H. Griffin, and also designed and marked the route from the summit to Boo Tarn.

My suggested route returns along the main ridge, over Brim Fell, to Swirl How (NY 27280/00550, elevation 802m (2630ft)). (5). At Swirl How take the path east, down Prison Band, to the large cairn at the bottom. Instead of walking along the path back to Levers Water drop down to the stream, Swirl Hause Beck, to the right of the path. Amble along the side of this pleasant beck. On the right side of the stream is the engine from an aircraft, an Anson, which crashed in 1944, killing the three aircrew (NY 27763/00143). There is more wreckage higher up the hillside and I found a piece of metal nearer the reservoir (NY 27772/00006).

The beck leads back to Levers Water, but on the way you may visit a trap for foxes and a small ruin (SD 27640/99700). To get there, contour below the scree, SE of Great How Crags. The goose bield, so called because a goose was used as bait, is a beehive-shaped structure (SD 27650/99780). The fox walked along a plank that collapsed, trapping it.

Walk down to Levers Water (6) and go round the eastern side of the reservoir. Cross the dam and inspect the deep shafts of Simon's Nick copper mine. Recently a team from the University College of London explored the mine looking for a tunnel(s) that has been 'lost'. Go south, up the short slope past the mine into Boulder Valley and back to the Pudding Stone (7).

A path leads back to the car park. Near here, is a rock with a memorial plaque to 'Joyce'. Close to Boo Tarn are a pile of stones, several heavy metal plates and cogs for winding (SD 28340/96680). By the road, on the descent to Coniston, are a tunnel and a pit for a mill waterwheel (SD 297974).

The Sun Hotel, further down the hill, is an ideal pub for refreshments. It is where the Fell & Rock Club held its first meeting in 1906. There are old photographs of Donald Campbell and Bluebird. The beer includes Hawkshead bitter, Bluebird and Black Cat.

## *Note:*

In 1958 the Aetherius Society classed the Old Man of Coniston as a holy mountain, whose energy may be harnessed. Apparently, there are just 19 holy mountains in the World. Another one is Kinder Scout in the Dark Peak District. The society was founded in 1955 by a former London cabbie, George King.

# Walk 14. Crinkle Crags from Great Langdale

**Map:** OL6; map ref. prefix NY

**Distance:** 14km (9 miles)

**Ascent:** 1280m (4200ft)

**Time:** 7 hours

**Starting point/parking:** Car park by Old Dungeon Ghyll Hotel, free for NT members (286060). Alternatively, there are spaces by the road near Side Pike.

## General Description

The ascent to Crinkle Crags is directly up the fell to the northernmost Crinkle. There is the option of a scramble up Hell Gill. The route takes in the five Crinkle Crag tops and continues to Pike o'Blisco. It then crosses Wrynose Fell and descends to Blea Tarn. The way along the Crinkles and to Pike o'Blisco is on paths. After Pike o'Blisco there is some pathless terrain. A waterfall, Whorneyside Force, and the site of an aircraft crash are visited. Malc, Tony H. and I did this walk on a pleasant September day.

## Route

From the Old DG take the track to Stool End Farm. Turn left immediately after the farm to walk above Oxendale Beck, to the footbridge opposite Crinkle Gill (263052) (1). At the footbridge leave the path and use the stream bed to get to the lovely waterfall of Whorneyside Force. (In the first minute I slipped, fell in the water and got soaked.) At the bottom of the waterfall climb the steep, grassy bank on the left to the path above. Take this to the bottom of the Hell Gill ravine.

Hell Gill is classed as a Grade 1 scramble. On this visit it seemed more difficult but I did have a bad start! If you don't want to scramble up Hell Gill go west to the gill that comes down from north of High Bleaberry Knott (25780/05270).

The noise of the water echoing around the walls in Hell Gill adds to the atmosphere. Getting past the first, deep pool in the gill is the trickiest part. Traverse along the right wall, above a deep pool, with a couple of long steps. The next fall is climbed on the right. A 12ft fall is bypassed on the left, up mossy rocks. Climb up to the left of a large boulder, left of the next fall, and down the other side. The route becomes easier. Pass under a large rowan tree on the left. The last waterfall before the exit requires a step, on the left of the fall, across a deep pool, then a move up mossy rocks. The ravine splits into two. There is no way out of the left branch, which ends with a high waterfall. The right branch is also a dead-end. One possible exit angles back on the right side of the ravine. We used the steep nose between the two branches. Start along the right branch and immediately climb up the nose on your left. Go up, crossing to the other side of the nose. Continue up the centre on loose rock and grass. The route requires care because of the exposure. At the top, continue along the side of the gill for 150m and then cross it to the west side.

Leave the stream and contour SW towards the gill to the north of High Bleaberry Knott (25500/05300). This gill goes west, directly towards the bottom of the 1st Crinkle. Climb alongside the gill, past Low and High Bleaberry Knotts.

In 1937 a Vildebeeste, a torpedo-bomber biplane, crashed in this area. We searched for anything that might resemble wreckage and found a small piece of thin metal by a large boulder (25222/05220, elevation about 600m (2000ft)). We also found a piece of wire (25190/05206), 1m long, a piece of wood with red paint and the burnt-looking sole of a boot (25162/05201). The highest metal fragment is 30m left of the base of the buttress (25075/05170). Climb up a grassy tongue to the right of the scree, aiming for the col immediately to the north of the 1st Crinkle, Gunson Knott (24970/05220).

It is possible to scramble up the east buttress of Gunson Knott but the rock is rather loose. I started 20m left of the lowest part of the buttress, along a ledge that slopes right. This leads to the right edge. Go left, then go up a groove with loose scree and climb rocks to the top, not far from the summit.

The 1st Crinkle, named Gunson Knott has no cairn (24994/05152) (2). In cloud the tops of the Crinkles are tricky to distinguish and it is easy to go off route. In poor visibility, walkers crossing the Crinkles from the south often get lost and find themselves to the west, below

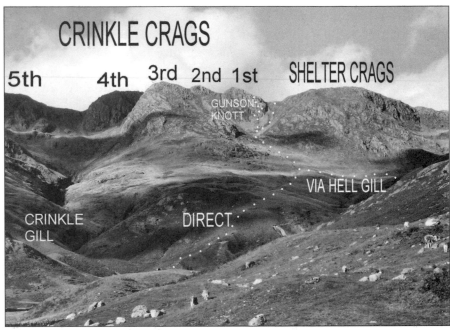

Crinkle Crags

the Three Tarns, in Eskdale. (I've done this a couple of times. If you get lost in this part of the Lakes it's a safe bet that you're in Eskdale!)

The 2nd Crinkle, 90m to the south and 10m east of the path, is higher (24978/05064).

Continue to the 3rd Crinkle, a further 90m to the south and 40m east of the path (25006/04982). Cross the gap of Mickle Door to the 4th Crinkle, named Long Top. This is 180m SW of the 3rd Crinkle and is the highest (24867/04873). There are several cairns. Go 100m southwards from the summit, past a lower cairn, to the famous Bad Step, where boulders block a gully. When I first did the Crinkles, decades ago, it was possible to squeeze through gaps between the jammed boulders. For years it was blocked. Then, surprisingly, a couple of years ago it was again possible to get through. On this latest visit, after descending by the Bad Step, I managed to climb back up through the gaps between the boulders. It helps if you're thin! When you put your head in the first hole the way out is hidden. You need to force your way up, with a little difficulty, to see the exit. From the Bad Step

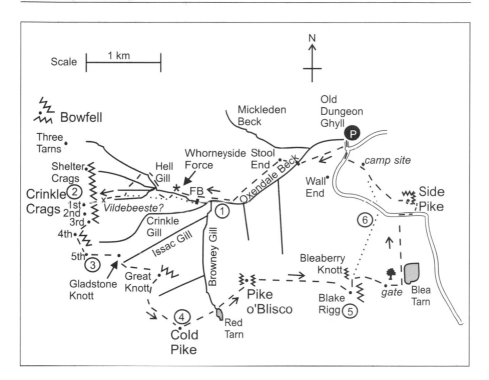

continue southwards for 300m to the 5th Crinkle (25005/04555) (3). According to an old guidebook by Bagley, it used to have the name Flesk on OS maps.

Head eastwards towards Great Knott. For good views leave the path and go along the northern edge by Gladstone Knott, north of a small tarn to Great Knott (25960/04270, elevation 696m (2283ft)). Looking back as you go along the edge, you may see Gladstone's Finger, a pinnacle of rock that juts out below the edge.

To go to Cold Pike contour SW then head SE to a path by a fence. At a stile by Cold Pike a notice explained that this electric fence was to stay until Jan 2007 to help re-establish the 'heaf' of sheep lost after the 'foot and mouth' outbreak in 2001. It also warned that, within a range of 30m, compasses might be affected (an excuse to remember!). Cold Pike has a rocky top with fine views. (26290/03610, elevation 701m (2300ft)) (4).

From the summit, drop NE to the crossroads north of Red Tarn. Iron was once mined in this area and there is a fenced-off shaft at the bottom of the path to Pike o'Blisco. Tony took the path back to the Old DG whilst Malc and I headed up to the Pike. The summit has two cairns, the highest to the NW (27120/04210, elevation 705m (2313ft)).

A path goes east from a point near the lower cairn and drops down through crags. Take this for 700m to a cairn where the path begins to drop down towards a gully (27800/04200). Go east, off-path, over Wrynose Fell. Near Bleaberry Knott follow a path to Blake Rigg (28510/03910) (5). (We saw a pair of buzzards circling above the cairn.)

To the east are steep crags but a grassy slope descends to the north, passing below Bleaberry Knott. Take this, aiming for Harrison Stickle in the distance and continue to the bottom of a grassy gully (28530/04310). The easiest way from here, avoiding bracken on the lower slopes, is keep going down on a bearing of 020°, to the road by Side Pike. We chose to visit Blea Tarn, which meant going eastwards towards a wall (28700/04350). Then we struggled downhill for 300m, through bracken and rocks, to a gate in the wall (28970/04260). After the gate, a pleasant path goes through the wood to Blea Tarn, *so placed, to be shut out from all the world!* (Wordsworth). Two seats overlook the tarn and the view makes up for previous effort. West of the tarn, a path goes north to the road below Side Pike (6). On the other side of this road a track snakes down, through the campsite to the Old DG.

In my youth, the first hill I climbed in the Lakes was Side Pike. Strangely, I hadn't visited it since so, whilst Malc headed down, I couldn't resist a short detour.

To finish with Side Pike, go east for 300m along the road, to a path by a fence (293051). This leads up to a stile near the wall along the col, to the east of Side Pike. Over the stile a good path leads to 'Fat Man's Agony', a gap between a boulder and the crag. (I did notice a 'cheat's' route beyond the gap!) The path continues to the summit cairn where I was reminded of the days of my first visit (29310/05370, elevation 363m (1193ft)). An easy path heads westwards, back to the road. Just before this, take a sheep track downhill, through bracken, to a wide track leading to the campsite and the Old DG. Tony and Malc were in this classic walkers'/climbers' pub. A pint of Black Sheep went down very quickly.

# Walk 15. Bowfell and Esk Pike from Cockley Beck

**Map:** OL6; map ref. prefix NY

**Distance:** 15km (9.5 miles)

**Ascent:** 1030m (3400ft)

**Time:** 7 hours

**Starting point/parking:** Opposite the bridge at Cockley Beck (east side) there is space for two to three cars, by the signpost (247016). I can remember, as a child, that there used to be a gate across the road over the bridge; there was a 6 penny toll to open it.

## General Description

The route goes up to Little Stand and Stonesty Pike then passes below Crinkle Crags to Bowfell. It continues to Esk Pike and returns down Mosedale. Much of the route is off-path. Even after a dry spell the ground lower down is boggy, but after rain … . It is safer to choose a day when the cloud ceiling is above 750m (2500ft) for the section below Crinkle Crags. There are possibilities for easy scrambling (these can be avoided) and an aircraft wreck site is near the route.

A couple of years ago Tony, Brian and myself arrived at Cockley Beck. It had been raining for days and I'd forgotten my boots. My trainers became waterlogged in the first 50m. On a recent trip in spring, the weather was cold, clear and sunny. Pools of water were iced over but the rock was dry and provided good holds.

## Route

Cross the road bridge over the River Duddon, and turn right immediately. Climb a stile, 15m from the bridge, to gain the riverbank, cross a footbridge over Mosedale Beck and climb a stile back over the wall (or simply paddle across the ford). It is possible to go north, directly to Little Stand by crags that provide scramble routes. However, I suggest that you use the crags closer to Gaitscale Gill for the ascent as these provide easier scrambles on good rock. (If you wish to avoid scrambling it is easy to work your way between the crags to reach Little

The view from Litlle Stand

Stand.) Continue eastwards by the fence for just over 1km (25540/02040). Go up the fell to a gate (25560/02240). Continue north to one of two stiles by the corner of the field. (On the spring day I saw my first skylarks and wheatears of the year.)

A series of small crags lie between here and Little Stand. They face south, so they dry quickly. I suggest you choose your own route but I will try to describe the way I took.

I climbed a small crag on the right to a perched block (25495/02560). I went right, to the bottom of a rock wall, climbed this and then went to the foot of a steep knott (25325/02725). After a tricky start, the rocks are at an easier angle. Two crags, with horizontal lines, are split by a grassy gully. I chose the left-hand one. The front is steep so I started 2m inside the gully (25240/02970). Above, there is easy scrambling. I went left to a nasty looking wall (25170/03135) and climbed to the right of centre where there are good holds. The cairn at the top of Little Stand comes into sight and looking back, there are

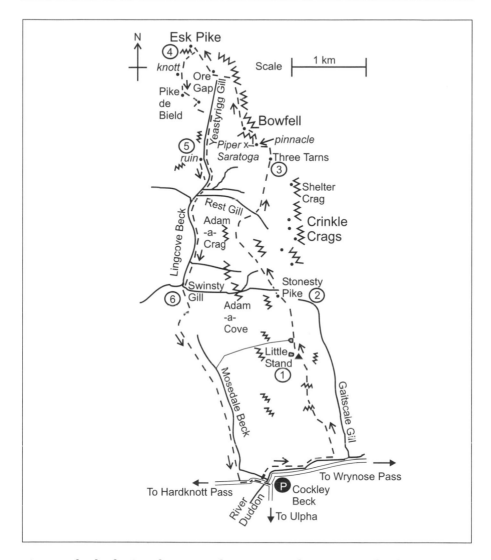

views of Black Combe, Devoke Water (the tarn with the greatest surface area in the Lakes) and the coast. Walk to the cairn (25050/ 03380) (1). On the map a triangle indicates a trig point. On my bootless trip we spent ages in the mist looking for a concrete pillar. Eventually we found a small brass bubble fixed to the rock. On the more recent visit I couldn't find this marker but I hope this failure was due to poor eyesight.

Head north, past a small pool to Stonesty Pike, 700m away. There is a cairn at 25120/04050 but Stonesty Pike is further west, on the opposite side of several pools (24940/04120, elevation 765m (2510ft)) (2).

The next target is Three Tarns between Crinkle Crags and Bowfell. A way can be found which contours below Crinkle Crags on the west side. This is mainly on grass, with some loose scree and off-path apart from the occasional sheep track. The elevation stays between 650m and 680m. In cloud, it is difficult to determine whether to go above or below crags and could be dangerous. On a clear day it is safe and gives fine views across to the Scafells. From Stonesty Pike take a bearing of 300° for 400m, crossing a gill and descending slightly to pass below a crag. In 2006 there was an electric fence to step over (see later). Contour round for 800m, on grassy slopes and go below a crag (24310/04910). Go north across loose scree, passing below a large boulder, scramble up rocks for about 20m and contour round the deep sides of Rest Gill (24700/05200). Continue on grass slopes, rising gently to a path (24650/05610). This leads to the Three Tarns (3).

From here, the choice is either the path to Bowfell or an easy scramble up Bowfell Links. For the scramble and to find aircraft wreckage, go up the Bowfell path for 200m then turn left below the crags. Go 250m across the top of the screes. An obvious rock pinnacle marks the bottom of the scramble (24550/06260). The engine of a small aircraft lies 50m further on (24504/06268). It is from a Piper Saratoga that crashed in 1987; there is more wreckage scattered on the scree below.

The scramble, Grade 1, starts at the pinnacle. Scramble up the rock directly behind the pinnacle, keeping a small gully to the left. Where the first rock stage ends, move a few metres right, round a short wall. The scrambling is enjoyable but it is only a short distance to the top of the buttress. Join the main path up to the summit of Bowfell (24470/06440, elevation 902m (2960ft)).

Leave the summit, heading just to the left of north to take the main path to Ore Gap. In cloud, it isn't easy to find the start of the path but, to help, there is a cairn (24460/06570). After this, the route is well marked. From Ore Gap follow the path west, then NW to Esk Pike. The summit rock is just SW of a large cairn (23660/07520, elevation 885m (2903ft)) (4).

The Pinnacle, Bowfell Links

Once, from here, I mixed up red and black on my compass and led my group south into Eskdale when we wanted to go north to Esk Hause. We lost several hundred feet in height before I realised my mistake. My attempt to cover up, by contouring round, failed to deceive my friends.

Go SE from the summit of Esk Pike for a few metres (there is a crag due south), then go south. In this direction there are three knotts, one of which is Pike de Bield. Go to the first rocky knott, by the cairn is a small memorial plaque to a Gerry Charnley (23620/07070). Walk south to a slightly lower knott, which I think is Pike de Bield (23600/06840, elevation 810m (2657ft)). Then, go eastwards to a third knott (23690/06790). Drop SW for 100m off this small peak, then go east, to a ruined wall, near Yeastyrigg Gill.

Follow the gill or use the stream bed to descend below Yeastyrigg Crags. Tucked behind a huge boulder is an old shelter (23780/06100). The walls and chimney are still intact but the building is roofless. The location and view are magnificent (5). A grassy path leads south to Green Hole where the stream is now Lingcove Beck. At some point you need to cross to the east bank. Follow this delightful beck for 1km, past some pools that would be tempting on a hot day. (Along here, I once disturbed a buzzard feasting on carrion.)

Swinsty Gill joins from the east (you crossed this gill higher up, near Stonesty Pike). On the south side of the gill, a path heads over to Mosedale (23590/04370) (6). If you miss it you will end up in Eskdale and will have to walk over Hardknott Pass to get back to Cockley Beck. The path goes uphill, gaining 40m in height, before dropping into Mosedale. In 2006 there was a stile over an electric fence (a continuation of the one that we crossed earlier). A notice said that the fence was temporary and that its purpose was to re-establish the ability of sheep to stay in their own heaf (historical grazing area). This is because farmers needed to restock after the foot and mouth outbreak in 2001.

The path goes along the west side of Mosedale and comes out at the bottom of Hardknott Pass, with the bridge over Cockley Beck 400m to the left. Even in good conditions Mosedale is one of the boggiest places in the Lakes. On my bootless day, my feet had squelched non-stop whilst Tony boasted that his were dry, so I deliberately led him through the worst ground I could find. Back at the car, when Tony took off his size 12 boots, his socks were still bone-dry. After Mosedale on a very wet day that was impressive: my trainers were cleaner than they'd been in years. We drove down the Duddon valley to the Newfield Inn, one of my favourite Lakeland pubs. An alternative is the Blacksmiths Arms at Broughton Mills. I recall going there in the 1960s when the beer came from a jug and the room had a single, large square table that everyone sat round.

### Note:

A journalist, John Pepper, spent several winters in this area and wrote a book, *Cockley Beck*, which describes life and characters in the Duddon Valley. He lived in the small room at the end of the farm at Cockley Beck.

# Walk 16. Great Carrs and Wetherlam from Tilberthwaite

**Maps:** OL6, OL7

**Distance:** 17.5km (11 miles)

**Ascent:** 1200m (3940ft)

**Time:** 8¼ hours

**Starting point/parking:** Take the minor road to Tilberthwaite, off the A593, 3km north of Coniston. There is a large car park by Yewdale Beck (NY 306010).

## General Description

The walk starts by visiting quarries on the way to the quiet Greenburn valley and then climbs up to Great Carrs. It continues over Swirl How to Wetherlam and returns to Tilberthwaite Gill, where there is the possibility of easy scrambling. Most of the walk is on paths apart from the upper Greenburn valley. Various quarries, mines and a cave are investigated (a short rope is useful to help climb down 2m into the cave). It is possible to walk through a tunnel (good torch needed). The site of an aircraft wreck is visited.

## Route

Continue along the road to the farm at High Tilberthwaite. Walk along the track through the gate on the left and follow this for 1km, past Knotts. Take a track that branches left (NY 30930/02270), and go 200m to a gate. Through the gate, turn right and look for a tunnel on the left (NY 30780/02430). If you wish to explore, it goes in for 15m to a supporting wall, then goes left for a further 5m.

Continue upwards on the mine track to the bottom of a slate quarry, where there is a stone shelter and seat (NY 30770/02500). This quarry may be investigated and it is possible to climb out at the southern end, to a second quarry. This is the one we're looking for, it contains a tunnel, at the northern end, known as Lanty Slee's cave (30691/02338) (1). He was famous for the illegal whisky he produced and supposedly had a still here. To reach it, go 20m along the left side and descend into the quarry. The cave is below a short rock face with

Abseiling in Black Hole Quarry

a wall above, at the very end of the quarry. There is a 6ft, rather slimy drop into the cave so the use of a short rope is advisable. The cave goes back for 15m but there isn't much to see apart from an old tyre and a pool of water.

Return to the main track from Tilberthwaite. The next diversion is to Black Hole Quarry near Slater Bridge. The easiest way is along the track past Atkinson Coppice. (Alternatively, go alongside the wall 150m east of the track and follow this to Slater Bridge. The woods on the other side of the wall are an interesting place to explore.) After 600m a track is reached (NY 306027), turn right and go past Low Hall Garth. The Yorkshire Ramblers Club have a cottage here, with a seat outside which has an inscription to a Herbert Thompson, 1914-2002.

150m past Slater Bridge turn right over a stile by a locked gate (NY 31370/02930). This leads to the entrance to Black Hole Quarry (sign-posted Cathedral Quarry) (2). Go through a short tunnel to enter the huge cavern and inspect its central pillar, then exit into the fresh air on the other side. You are likely to find people either abseiling down the sides of this slate quarry or climbing the bolted routes up

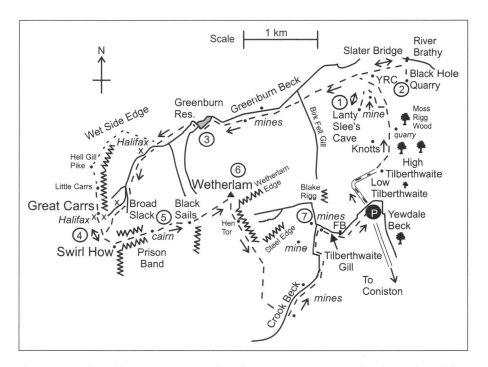

the vertical walls. Go up 5m of rocky steps to get to the far side of the quarry. If you go high up to the left, you will get a good view of the cavern entrance. Go down, below an overhanging face that is a popular abseil route, to a tunnel. This is wide and reasonably high and it leads to open air outside the quarry. Normally, I would not have entered the tunnel, but a large party of young school children had just gone ahead without the slightest whimper. So we went along it with a weak, wind-up torch, me clutching my comrade's rucksack. The tunnel bends in the middle, so there is no daylight for a short distance. A torch is essential and ideally helmets should be worn, look out for a low section of roof just before the exit! Return through the tunnel and the main cavern, back to the entrance to Black Hole Quarry. Go up the path to the left to a locked hut, and behind this is a short tunnel that leads to a platform high up in the main cavern.

After completing this exploration, return along the path past Low Hall Garth and 400m further on, take the left fork to the Greenburn valley. 200m past a wall, on the north side of the beck is a tunnel, the Greenburn Beck Level (NY 29320/02290). 2km up the valley, the ruins of old copper mine buildings are reached. There are several water-filled shafts but a large waterwheel pit is in good condition. (There are levels high up the hillside to the south. A friend has explored the Long Crag Level and gone about 100m into it (NY 28630/01540). He claims it is safe!) Continue up the valley to the broken dam wall of the reservoir that used to power the mine (3).

The target objective is Great Carrs. The easy way is to gain Wet Side Edge to the north, but much more interesting is to continue up the valley by the side of Greenburn Beck. Unless the ground is icy the steep slope up Broad Slack, south of Great Carrs, shouldn't be a problem. I have gone this way in winter with snow on the ground, when crampons would have been useful. Apart from the occasional sheep track there are no paths: there aren't many Lakeland valleys where this is the case. The beck flows through a small gorge then down a series of cascades but the rocks are too slimy for scrambling. There is a large sheepfold to the east of the beck and, on a spring day, a baby meadow pipit fluttered by my feet.

Follow the beck into Broad Slack. In the beck and on the hillside are large pieces of wreckage from a Halifax bomber that crashed in 1944. Seven Canadians and one Englishman were killed. Many walkers will have seen the memorial cairn and some of the undercarriage, on the top of the ridge near Great Carrs. Most of the wreckage was pushed over the edge and much has been removed to museums. Two engines have gone to the RAF Wyton museum; another lies outside the John Ruskin Museum in Coniston, where there is information about the accident. The first bit of wreckage I found was by the beck, below the cascades (NY 27711/01706). The remaining engine lies in the beck at an elevation of around 600m (NY 27320/00880). Larger pieces of wreckage, including two of the propeller bases, lie higher up (NY 27200/00800). More wreckage map references are given after the route description. Above the wreckage, continue up steeply to the ridge. I kept close to the crags on the right, by the side of the scree where grassy ledges make a reasonably easy ascent. On the ridge, turn right towards Great Carrs. Just before the summit, SW of the cairn is the memorial to the crew of the Halifax (27004/00811). Walk to the cairn on the top of Great Carrs (NY 27040/00920, 785m (2575ft)) (4).

Retrace your steps along the ridge and go south to the cairn at Swirl How (NY 27280/00550, elevation 802m (2630ft)). Descend the Prison

Halifax memorial, Great Carrs

Band to the cairn at the bottom (5). Climb the path towards Wetherlam and leave the path after 300m, (281009), to go directly to the summit of Black Sails (NY 28290/00755, elevation 745m (2443ft)).

Go NE across grassy slopes to the top of Wetherlam (NY 28830/01100, elevation 762m (2502ft)) (6). From the cairn go south, keeping close to the left edge of the ridge for excellent views of Tilberthwaite. There are also views of Windermere, Coniston, Esthwaite Water and Morecambe Bay. Hen Tor, by a small tarn 300m from Wetherlam, is marked with a cairn. On each side of Hen Tor there are gullies dropping down towards Tilberthwaite. The Harris Museum and Art Gallery in Preston has a 1921 painting, by W.G. Collingwood, of Hen Tor with snow in the gullies. There is also a painting of his, of Wetherlam, at Ruskin's old Coniston home, Brantwood.

Go southwards to a cairn above a pool, continue south on a pleasant path for approx. 700m and then take a path that branches left (SD 29160/99670). It descends gently to join the path along Crook Beck by a reedy pool (SD 29500/99300).

Turn NE towards Tilberthwaite. There are copper mine workings near this path and a cave filled with water that may conceal a shaft (SD 29640/99400). Further along, on the other side of the beck there is a deep, sloping gash. The mine track leads to Tilberthwaite Gill. Here, cross Crook Beck and go to the footbridge, at the top of the gill, where there is a mine tunnel entrance, Benson's Lode Level (NY 29940/00800) (7).

There are paths above the gill on each side that go back to the car park but if you want to explore along the gill, walk back along the south side until you are past the top waterfall (NY 29974/00737). Go down the bank to the floor of the ravine. To the left of the waterfall is a tunnel, Gill Head Waterfall Level. The gill provides an easy scramble and a path has been formed in places. This was a popular place to visit in Victorian times, when walkways where built on the side of the ravine. After 300m, by a dead tree on the right, the gill steepens, the gorge narrows and a waterfall, with a large rock across the top, plunges into a deep pool. It is time to retreat! Go back about 50m and on the south side of the gill there is an obvious escape route up the bank. Continue through bracken, to the main path. This drops down to a spot above a quarry with steep walls, another popular place for outdoor activity groups.

Turn left at a junction to return to the gill near a footbridge. If you go back up the gill, to below the waterfall, you will see why it is unsafe to come down. The rock on the left wall is one way but it is particularly greasy, classed as a Grade 2 scramble. I climbed up once and found it quite tricky. Either walk easily down Yewdale Beck, or investigate the slate quarry area, as you return to the car park. (I saw a pair of grey wagtails along the beck.)

In the field opposite the car park, there is a sheepfold. It contains sculptures by the artist Andy Goldsworthy.

The Crown Inn and Black Bull Inn, in Coniston are both good pubs.

### Note:

Map references of more aircraft wreckage: NY 27530/01280, NY 27480/01120, NY 27480/01060, NY 27443/01014, NY 27393/00948, NY 27227/00800, and NY 27170/00780.

# Walk 17. Hard Knott and Harter Fell from the Duddon Valley

**Map:** OL6

**Distance:** 20km (12.5 miles); (17.5km (11 miles) without Green Crag)

**Ascent:** 1300m (4260ft); (1130m (3700ft) without Green Crag)

**Time:** 9 hours; (8 hours without Green Crag)

**Starting point/parking:** Car park 4km north of Seathwaite, by the road to Cockley Beck (SD 235995).

## General description

This route goes to Hard Knott, then past Hardknott Fort and over Harter Fell. There is the option of visiting Crook Crag and Green Crag. It returns past Wallowbarrow Crag and along the River Duddon. The route before Harter Fell is mainly off-path, over some boggy ground. Afterwards it is mainly on paths, though these are on awkward rocky and boggy terrain, making progress slow. There are opportunities for scrambling. Features of interest include a hill fort, the Eskdale Needle, Hardknott Fort and the attractive River Duddon. Malc and I did this walk at the end of October and, due to a late start, were pushed for time.

## Route

Cross the bridge over the River Duddon, immediately turn right along the riverbank and go over boggy ground for 30m to a good path. After 1km a rocky knoll, Castle How is reached; this is thought to be the site of a hill fort. The sides are steep but the top may be reached from the west. Continue on the path to Black Hall Farm, where the line of the old Roman road is crossed. Go over two stiles, to a path that goes north to a bridge on the Hardknott Pass road (1). Hardknott Gill flows through a culvert under the bridge. Join the gill on the far side of the bridge and scramble up its bed. A Grade 1 scramble, there are no real difficulties and it is a pleasant way to gain height. When we were there, recent rain meant there was a lot of water, so a couple of small waterfalls and a small, narrow gorge were quite entertaining. We

The view from Hard Knott

bypassed a 10ft fall (NY 23220/01640) and shortly afterwards left the gill, near a ruined wall. Step over a wire fence and walk to the crags on the left, above the road (NY 23080/01580). South facing, the rock provides a short, easy scramble to a cairn at the top.

Walk past a pretty tarn to the summit of Border End (NY 22830/01880). Another cairn, to the north gives views over Eskdale. Take a path that winds its way to the summit of Hard Knott, 600m away, bearing 035°, (NY 23190/02360, elevation 549m (1801ft)) (2).

(Malc decided to preserve as much height as possible, so headed back towards the top of Hardknott Pass and took the path from there to Harter Fell.) My route involves an extra 150m loss of height, and going off-path over some boggy ground. The next objective is the Eskdale Needle, not as exciting as Napes Needle but worth seeing. To get there, go west for 350m, dropping down between crags. The Needle, or Steeple, is just below a crag, the rock in between having eroded to leave a detached pinnacle (NY 22810/02420).

After inspecting the Needle, contour south, then west to a point below the Border End crags (NY 22370/02080). Continue SW and, as

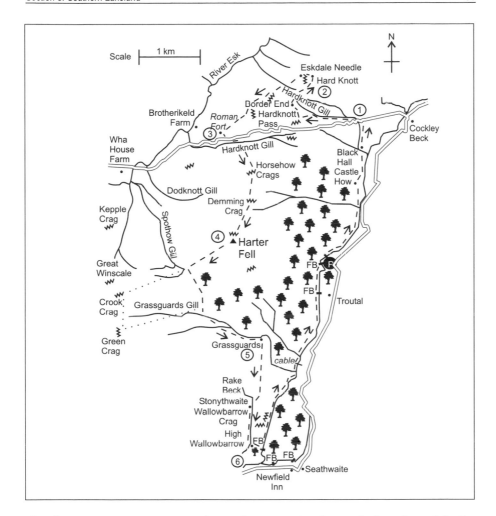

the fort comes into view, drop down to it, through bracken (3). Its Roman name was Mediobognvm; notice the parade ground, with a platform for the leaders, 250m NE of the walls of the actual fort.

Cross the road by the car park and go to another Hardknott Gill, stepping over a fence on the way. Walk east, above the gill, until past the gorge (NY 22190/01360). Cross the gill and head 400m to the bottom of Horsehow Crags, bearing 160° (NY 22350/00930). (On the way, look back for impressive views of the fort.) These north-facing crags are rather slippery and not ideal for scrambling, but give some

Eskdale Needle

sport as height is gained. Go up steep grass to the left of a vertical face. Above, it is possible to scramble steeply up a mixture of heather and boulders. At the top, go south for 250m and climb over a gate in a fence. Walk to the bottom of Demming Crag, a further 250m from the fence (NY 22270/00300).

An obvious rake/gully climbs diagonally left to right across the face. Go steeply up this, until there is a break in the rock face on the left. Go through this until you are below a perched rock. Climb up, to the right of this and traverse left, past the rock, to the east side of the crag, not far from the main Harter Fell path. Climb to the top, on good rock, and walk uphill to Harter Fell. Go through a break in the crag's north face and scramble to the summit on the right (SD 21880/99720, elevation 653m (2142ft)) (4). Malc had arrived shortly before me and was sat by the trig point, tucking into his lunch.

Leave the summit on a path that starts west then heads, on 230°, in the direction of Crook Crag. At the bottom of the slope there is the option of including Crook Crag and Green Crag in the walk. This involves crossing boggy ground to get to the short, enjoyable scrambles up the rocky pikes, and then crossing more boggy ground, to a stile near the edge of the forest (SD 21310/98530). On that October day, we didn't have the time for this diversion, but I have enjoyed these pikes on previous occasions.

At the bottom of Harter Fell turn left, through a gate, along an awkward forest path.

Fork right at a junction (SD 21410/98860). Continue south for 300m to a gate (no fence!) by the top of Grassguards Gill (SD 21450/98590). Go past a sign, 'Public Bridlepath to Eskdale' (I pity a poor horse on these paths) and follow the gill along a very muddy path to Grassguards (5). A path goes round the farm, where a rather fetching pink Land Rover was parked. There is a short cut to the River Duddon on the far side of Grassguards Gill but, time permitting, take a good track southwards, for over 1km, to Wallowbarrow Crag.

At Stonythwaite turn left (arrowed) and go south, by Wallowbarrow Crag. As we went past, we saw a climber just finishing his route. Drop down to High Wallowbarrow and turn left by the farm, along a path signposted Seathwaite. After 300m, a bridge over the River Duddon is reached (6). The Newfield Inn is a tempting 500m away but better to save it for later.

It is just over 3km, along the west side of the river, back to the car park. There are cascades, waterfalls and, at the right time of year, you may see a pair of peregrine falcons that nest along the gorge by Wallowbarrow Crag. Unfortunately, the path manages to be both rocky and boggy, demanding attention when you would rather be taking in the scenery. An interesting crossing over the river is met; this is by using stepping-stones whilst hanging onto a steel cable. The rocks were submerged, so we declined this invitation. A footbridge to Troutal is passed, before reaching a bridge back to the car park.

We drove the short distance to the Newfield Inn, which had beer from a brewery in Hawkshead, Cumbrian Legendary Ales, including King Dunmail and Wicked Jimmy. I thoroughly enjoyed a pint of the latter. Notice the slate floor, from Walna Scar Quarry; the dark lines are volcanic ash from successive eruptions, millions of years ago.

# Walk 18. Scafell and Scafell Pike from Eskdale

**Map:** OL6; map ref. prefix NY

**Distance:** 23.5km (14.5 miles)

**Ascent:** 1540m (5100ft)

**Time:** 10¼ hours

**Starting point/parking:** Small car park, opposite Wha House Farm, on the Eskdale to Hardknott Pass road (200009). Alternatively, east of phone box, near a cattle grid (212011).

## General Description

The route starts with a scenic walk past tarns to Great How. It goes over Slight Side to the Scafells and returns along Eskdale. The way up to Scafell and the return along the River Esk valley are 'far from the madding crowd'. Most of the route is on good paths. The sites of several aircraft wrecks and the two highest tarns in the Lakes may be visited.

## Route

Walk west along the road to the Woolpack Inn. Take the footpath between the Inn and the farm, sign-posted 'Burnmoor & Wasdale Head'. Go past a stile and signs to Boot and the Woolpack Inn. A ruin, in good condition apart from being roofless, is passed 30m on your left. Cross a muddy area on stepping-stones and turn right. After 1km picturesque Eel Tarn is reached (1). Go round its south side and join the path NE to Stony Tarn (191019). For a good view of the tarn, go to a grassy knoll 30m to the right of the path.

Continue for 1km and then leave the path, and go NW to the rarely visited Great How. Very little extra ascent is involved and there are excellent views of Harter Fell, Eskdale and the coast. By the summit cairn is a 'bubble' trig point (19740/04000, elevation 522m (1713ft)) (2). Burnmoor Tarn lies just to the west, below the steep edge. Having made Great How's day, head NE towards Slight Side across Quagrigg Moss. A sheep track goes most of the way and surprisingly, when I

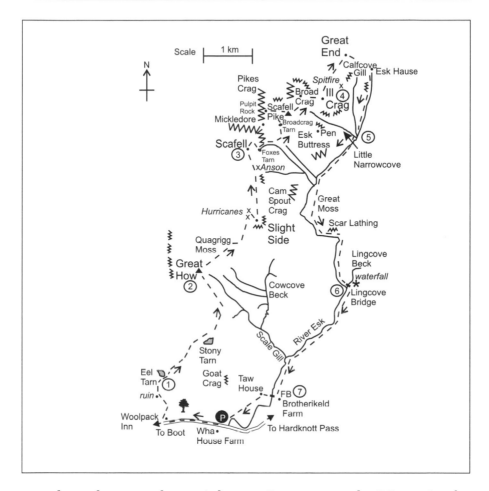

was there the ground wasn't boggy. Once across the Moss, aim for boulders to the east and regain the main path, (20800/04400), to Slight Side.

In 1941 two fighter aircraft, Hurricanes, flew into Horn Crag below Slight Side. There are two separate wreck sites, one of which is marked by a cross (20850/05040 & 20810/05165). Sadly, the memorial plaque to the Polish pilots has disappeared. Go to the rocky tor on Slight Side (20980/05020, elevation 762m (2499ft)).

Walk north over Long Green towards Scafell. 500m before the summit, at the top of a steep rise, there is a cairn and 20m to the east,

Burnmoor Tarn from the north-east

is wreckage from an aircraft, an Anson that crashed in 1943 (20845/06170) (see Walk 12). Continue to Scafell summit (20680/06480, elevation 964m (3162ft)) (3). The path continues north, past a shelter. The objective is to go to Scafell Pike via Foxes Tarn. The path down starts by a cairn (20790/06630). It descends steeply to the small tarn, the second highest in the Lakes. (Once, in winter, I saw a flock of snow buntings in this fine corrie.) From the tarn, follow the outflow down to the main scree shoot below Mickledore (21160/06600).

Rather than going up the scree, go east, and then climb north to Broadcrag Tarn, the highest tarn in the Lake District (21310/06920, elevation 837m (2746ft)). The area between here and the summit was the site of a stone-axe factory. Continue NW to the main path to Scafell Pike. A short diversion towards Pulpit Rock to the west of the path is worthwhile for the excellent views (20970/07140). Several well-constructed shelters lie to the west of Scafell Pike. Apart from

Lingcove Bridge, Eskdale

the summit platform there is a trig point (21540/07230, elevation 978m (3210ft)).

From the cairn, drop down to the north and go up, past Broad Crag. Go right, off the path, to visit Ill Crag (22320/07350, elevation 935m (3067ft)) (4). Continue along the ridge to the north of Ill Crag. In 1947 a Spitfire, a fighter aircraft, crashed 20 feet from the top. There is a small amount of wreckage and a memorial plaque (22505/07714). After the accident, it was 6 months before the wreckage was found.

If the weather is clear you may wish to visit Great End for the superb views from the western edge. If you do, after leaving Great End, head SE on a path that rejoins the main one between Scafell Pike and Esk Hause (a point on the path is 22800/08200). The plan is to walk down the Esk valley. Either go down by Calfcove Gill (start at 228080) or continue to the cairn at Esk Hause and take the path southwards, on the west side of the gill (232081).

After the crowds, it is a delightful and peaceful walk down the valley. Cross the beck from Littlenarrow Cove and then go over to the east side of the River Esk (5). There are good views of Pen, Cam Spout Crag and Esk Buttress, a climbing area. A path cuts across the Great Moss (look for a large boulder). Some walkers choose the slightly shorter route, above the crags to the west of the river but the path along the water is prettier.

Continue alongside the river, by a right-angled bend below Scar Lathing. A few stepping-stones cross a gill (22570/04720). I saw a tent here, pitched by someone who likes solitude. The river now flows down a ravine with lovely cascades and pools. On the distant skyline the Eskdale Needle comes into view. At Lingcove Bridge the River Esk meets Lingcove Beck, near a waterfall and tempting pools (6).

Continue on the path by the river. Don't get dragged uphill by the main path but stay down by the water (223028). Cross two stiles and walk along the fence. Cross a stile back over the fence and climb another one over a wall on the right. Go through fields (path ill-defined), to a pair of gates. The left one is to Brotherikeld Farm, the right one goes to a footbridge (7). (One winter's day, I saw an amazing number of chaffinches in the vicinity of the farm.) Cross the bridge and go through the field ahead to Taw House. Pass through a gate and turn left. Here, the heavens opened on me but I considered myself lucky to have stayed dry so long. The farm track goes to the road near the car park.

The Woolpack Inn, passed earlier, is the obvious choice for refreshment.

### Note:

Samuel Coleridge stayed at Taw House after his famous first descent of Broad Stand.

*Opposite: Aira Force (Walk 23)*

# Section 4: Eastern Lakeland

# Walk 19. Helvellyn from Wythburn

**Map:** OL5; map ref. prefix NY

**Distance:** 12.5km (8 miles)

**Ascent:** 1200m (3940ft)

**Time:** 6½ hours

**Starting point/parking:** Free car park by Wythburn Church, 0.5km from southern end of Thirlmere, off the A591 Ambleside to Keswick road (324136).

## General Description

The route goes past waterfalls and mines to Dollywaggon Pike, Nethermost Pike and Helvellyn. A circuit of Red Tarn by Swirral Edge and Striding Edge is optional. The return is along a rarely visited gill with considerable evidence of mining works. The way up and the descent are steep and off-path, but the ground isn't difficult. The rest of the route is on good paths. There are opportunities for easy scrambling. When I did this walk on a sunny day in February, the ground was frozen but there was no snow.

## Route

From the car park, take the main path for 300m towards Helvellyn, to a forest track that runs north–south. Turn right, sign-posted 'Dunmail Raise', and walk along this track, with fine views along Thirlmere, for just over 1km to Birkside Gill (1). Go through the gate before the bridge and follow the gill uphill. The first part consists of a lovely series of waterfalls and pools; the ice made the falls very attractive. In better conditions there may be the opportunity for some scrambling, particularly above the falls. To appreciate the waterfalls stay by the water, although there is a path by the forest fence. Notice an old copper mine next to the gill (32980/12590). The low wall at the entrance is easy to climb over and you may drop down a few feet to inspect the tunnel entrance. A torch is useful to see its construction. On the opposite side of the beck, 150m further on, is another entrance, covered by a metal grill through which may be seen a vertical shaft followed by a horizontal tunnel.

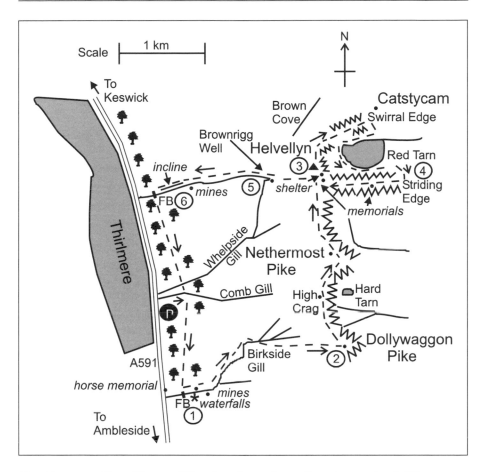

Continue up the gill, on either bank or along the stream bed. There are a few difficulties but these are easily bypassed. Where the gill emerges onto the fell, follow the right-hand branch, eastwards, towards Dollywaggon Pike. At the end of the gill continue to the summit (34610/13070, elevation 858m (2815ft)) (2). From the cairn, follow the edge of the cliffs northwards over High Crag (34330/13660, elevation 884m (2900ft)) to Nethermost Pike. On the way, keeping to the edge, look to the east for Hard Tarn, nestling below Nethermost Pike. Of the two cairns on Nethermost Pike, I made the northern one slightly higher (34370/14190, elevation 891m (2923ft)).

Follow the edge north towards Helvellyn (3). A stone, by a cairn, commemorates the landing of an aircraft by John Leeming and Bert

Hinkler on the mountain, on 22ⁿᵈ December 1926. A shelter is reached, (34260/15100), and the summit cairn is 20m further on (34240/15100 elevation 950m (3118ft)). Walk 100m NW to the trig point (34170/15160). (Often, ravens will be seen using the thermals above the edge.)

Red Tarn lies only 800 feet below, though it looks further away. If you have time to visit it, go northwards along the cliff for 120m to Swirral Edge. A cairn marks the top of the edge (34130/15270). Go down the arête and, at the lowest point, take the path that descends diagonally to the right. Leave the path halfway and go down to Red Tarn, elevation 718m (2356ft). Walk round the northern and then the western sides of the tarn, frozen on that day in February. Not many walkers go this way so there isn't a path. A small crag by the tarn has to be climbed and this is the perfect place for refreshment. The dam at the east side of the tarn was built to provide water for the Greenside lead mines. The next objective is to join Striding Edge.

An aircraft, a Mosquito, crashed below the Edge in 1945, killing the two Australian aircrew. In one of his books, W. Heaton Cooper mentions picking up a piece of wreckage by the tarn. There are a few very small fragments of molten metal and bolts 9m from Red Tarn (34880/15132). This is on the SE side of the tarn. I found another tiny fragment 80m above. There may be more debris higher up, nearer the point of impact.

From this (the SE) side of the tarn climb diagonally to join Striding Edge near its start (353151) (4). Scrambling along the arête, it is easy to miss the memorial to a Robert Dixon, who fell from this spot when following the Patterdale Foxhounds in 1858 (35000/14930). Continue along the ridge and up the steep face at the end. At the top, marking the point where the path descends to Striding Edge, is another memorial, to an artist, Charles Gough and his dog (34420/15000). He was killed in a fall below the memorial in 1805 and his faithful dog stayed by the body until it was found 3 months later.

Revisit the trig point and then descend for 400m, on a bearing of 250°, to Brownrigg Well (5) (33800/15060). This is one of the highest springs in Lakeland and produces a steady supply of water. Whelpside Gill flows south from the spring, but notice a narrow trench that has been dug near the start of the stream. This is a leat,

Red Tarn from Helvellyn

now dry, that was built to divert water to a lead mine. Follow the leat westwards for 250m to the top of a beck. This is unnamed on the map and the upper part is dry.

Continue down, alongside the beck, to a spoil heap and a small dam (6). This was built, along with the leat, to provide power for the mine. The water disappears underground and would have been used to drive a nearby waterwheel (32920/14980). There are signs of a mine entrance but this has been destroyed and only the walls and a piece of rail remain. To the south are ruined buildings and on the hillside above, you may see various spoil heaps from other tunnels that followed the vein of ore. Descend along the beck, and look for the remains of an iron wheel and cogs. On the south side, above another spoil heap and at the bottom of a gully, is a broken crankshaft. A mine incline runs on the north side of the beck, from below the waterwheel pit. The water-powered wheel would have winched materials up and down this slope. The top part is largely destroyed but the lower section is in excellent condition and provides a good track down.

Above a waterfall, cross to the south side of the beck. Continue down to a fence with a low, locked gate. Climb the gate and descend to the forest track below. Go south along this track for just over 1km. The signpost met earlier, points down to the car park. When I was there, the door of Wythburn Church was locked but you can walk round the outside of the building and peep though the windows.

Note: 1km south of the car park, on the wall on the east side of the A591, is a memorial to a horse (32520/12660). Dated 30/09/1843 the words are:

'FALL'N FROM HIS FELLOW'S SIDE
THE STEED BENEATH IS LYING
IN HARNESS, HERE HE DIED
HIS ONLY FAULT WAS DYING

After my walk, the Golden Rule in Ambleside provided much appreciated warmth and a pint of Hartley's.

# Walk 20. Dove Crag and Red Screes from Brothers Water

**Maps:** OL5, OL7; map ref. prefix NY

**Distance:** 15km (9.5 miles)

**Ascent:** 1100m (3670ft)

**Time:** 7 hours

**Starting point/parking:** Car park off A592, just north of Brothers Water (402134).

## General Description

The route goes up to Dove Crag by Hogget Gill. It continues by Scandale Pass to Red Screes and descends over Middle Dodd. Hogget Gill is a Grade 1 scramble and any tricky section can be bypassed. After Dove Crag the walk is on good paths. A cave on the face of Dove Crag may be visited and there is a mining area to explore. Malc, Tony and I did this when the gill was icy and there were snow squalls. I went back again in May to do more of the scramble up Hogget Gill.

## Route

From the car park take the path south, by the side of Brothers Water. Go past Hartsop Hall (mining area – see later) and keep by Dovedale Beck until the bottom of Hogget Gill, just before a footbridge (390114) (1). Cross the footbridge, or ford Dovedale Beck, and walk alongside Hogget Gill. 200m after the footbridge, on the far side of the gill, is a lead smelter, built in the 17th century. There are ruined walls and a couple of upright rocks (38870/11220). Continue to where the slope gets steeper.

On the icy trip we had to bypass several sections of Hogget Gill. I will describe my latest visit to the gill, when the rocks were greasy after heavy rain. I started up the right side of the first waterfalls and then went left near the top (38470/10840). A 15ft fall is reached (38370/10830). I passed this by climbing 2m to the right. A twin fall comes next; the rocks were slippery and I used tree roots on the right. A long waterslide in a trench provides a challenge. I clutched a

Dove Crag

branch and made an awkward manoeuvre over a boulder on the left, getting myself quite wet. A 25ft waterfall is bypassed on either side (38160/10720). Near the top, go straight ahead up the main branch. Good holds make the last fall easier than it looks. It is always possible to exit the stream and miss any sections that look difficult. (Near the end of the gill, I heard croaking and spotted two ring ouzels.) At the top of the scramble, you arrive on open hillside, by a wall (38030/10630) (2).

In poor visibility I would advise simply walking to the top of Dove Crag. However, if the visibility is good, the idea is to get a close look at the vertical climbing face of Dove Crag and visit a cave, Priest's Hole. To do this, follow the wall at the top of the gill north for 300m, then climb west, between crags, into a corrie, Hunsett Cove. Large boulders that have split off from Dove Crag lie in the corrie. Make your way, left of rocks, to the foot of the main face of the crag (37750/10960). Above is a classic VS climb of Don Whillans,

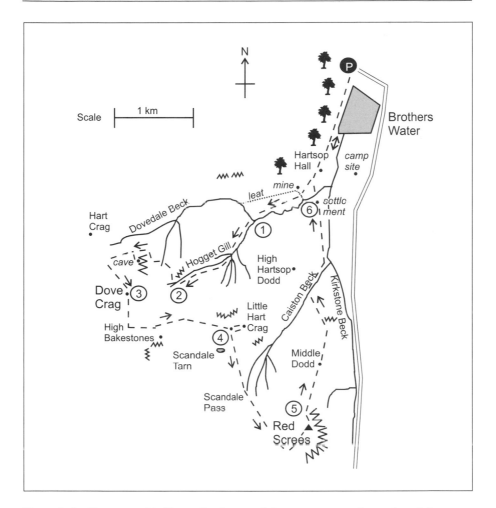

Dovedale Grooves. Follow the base of the crag, past huge boulders, to the col on the right (37580/11050). Go NW to meet the main path that comes up from Dovedale. To get to the cave, follow a thin track that goes left from the main path, by a large boulder. Climb up to the left by the side of scree (37560/11010). Here, the path becomes more defined and uses a shelf to access the cave (37590/10900). It is quite large and has a book for visitors to sign, but is not the place to spend a night if you are prone to sleepwalking. Return to the main path and climb up, swinging south to the summit of Dove Crag (37450/10430, elevation 792m (2598ft)) (3).

From the summit, take the path south for 400m to a cairn marking a junction (374100). In cloud, be careful not to miss this. Go east along a fence, dropping down over Bakestones Moss. From Black Brow, make a short diversion from the path, to climb the two rocky tors on Little Hart Crag (4).

Return to the main path and head southwards, along a wall to Scandale Pass. Cross the pass and ascend, by a wall, towards the top of Red Screes. At a junction of two walls, don't take the stony path SE but choose the grassy path that goes east (39240/08700). This leads directly to the summit trig point (39650/08760, elevation 776m (2546ft)) (5).

From the cairn, take a path heading just to the west of north, along the top of the steep east face of Red Screes. This goes down Smallthwaite Band to Middle Dodd. From here, keep going northwards, descending with excellent views of Brothers Water. On the way down it is necessary to drop west, off the ridge, to avoid a small, but vertical, crag. Go to a footbridge on the left, over Caiston Beck, from where a path goes to a bridge over Dovedale Beck and back to Hartsop Hall. Evidence of an ancient settlement is marked on the map, south of Hartsop Hall (398117) (6).

If you have time for exploration, a track, 20m before farm buildings, leads to disused lead mines and ruined buildings. There is a nasty looking, open tunnel with water on the floor, above a spoil heap. Just to the left of this, a leat joins a beck. This brought water, over 800m from Dovedale Beck, to provide power for the mine. Another dank tunnel is higher up.

For refreshment the Brotherswater Inn is a short drive towards the Kirkstone Pass or there is the White Lion, in Patterdale.

# Walk 21. Branstree and Harrop Pike from Sadgill

**Map:** OL7; map ref. prefix NY

**Distance:** 16km (10 miles)

**Ascent:** 890m (2930ft)

**Time:** 6¾ hours

**Starting point/parking:** Take the Longsleddale road off the A6, 6km north of Kendal. There is space for several cars to the east of the bridge at Sadgill (483057). **Note:** Driving down Longsleddale you pass a parking area and Public Conveniences, a thoughtful consideration.

## General Description

The walk goes up Longsleddale to the Gatescarth Pass and continues to Branstree and the top of Mosedale. Tarn Crag, Harrop Pike and Grey Crag are visited. It starts along a good track but later the paths are boggy and there are some pathless sections. The features include an interesting quarry, a bothy and several pillars that were built to help in the construction of the tunnel that carries water from Haweswater to Manchester. Tony accompanied me in February, in a cold wind with snow on the ground.

## Route

From Sadgill, walk up the valley with the River Sprint on your left. Buckbarrow Crag, on the right, has some rock climbing routes. After 3km, opposite a signpost, a stile on the left leads to Wrengill Quarry (477086) (1). This slate quarry, where World War 1 prisoners once worked, warrants a visit, so go over the stile and follow the path to the ruined buildings. An old engine lies on the ground and it is possible to go down to the quarry floor. Wren Gill enters the quarry as a water-fall, goes underground and re-emerges lower down. At the top of the workings there is a tunnel entrance (47213/08405). Over the wall to the north is an old pipeline.

Afterwards, return to the main track and continue to the top of Gatescarth Pass (474092). Go NE across boggy ground and follow the fence to the top of Branstree (2). A boundary stone with the letter 'L' is passed near the top. The summit cairn and a 'bubble' trig point are just to the north of the point where the fence meets a wall (47800/09960, elevation 713m (2339ft)).

The plan is to head for Grey Crag, but with a diversion to a bothy first. Walk 300m NE to a large cairn for fine views of Haweswater; unfortunately a snow squall spoilt the visibility when we were there (47980/10190).

Go east to another cairn and continue for a further 400m to a large

Tony by pipeline pillar on Branstree

stone pillar (48370/10260). This is one of the survey pillars marking the route of the first tunnel, built in 1936, to carry water nearly 100 miles from the Haweswater reservoir to Manchester. Mardale was flooded to form the reservoir, finished in 1940 and took two years to fill. From the pillar, go SE off-path down the fell and follow Great Grain Gill to Mosedale. Near the beck the ground is tussocky but towards the bottom you are rewarded with views of a small waterfall. 100m or so to the NE of the beck are extensive spoil heaps from a disused stone quarry.

At the bottom you will see Mosedale Cottage, now a well cared for, dry bothy. This makes a good place for a stop, particularly in poor weather (495095) (3). When we called there, two men were painting and carrying out other maintenance tasks. They invited us to enjoy

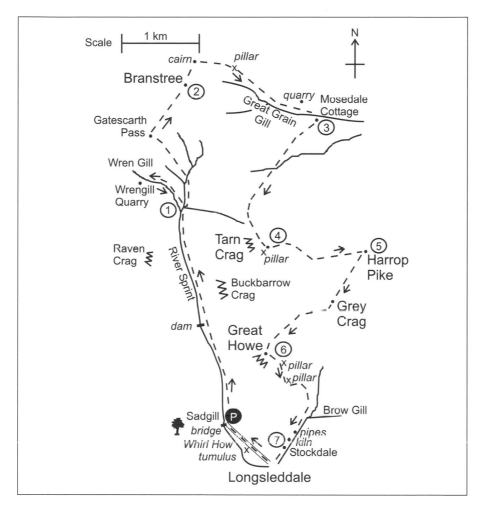

Scale |— 1 km —|

N

cairn — pillar

Branstree ②

quarry Mosedale

Great Grain Gill — Cottage ③

Gatescarth Pass

Wren Gill

Wrengill Quarry ①

Raven Crag

River Sprint

Tarn Crag ④
pillar

⑤ Harrop Pike

Buckbarrow Crag

Grey Crag

dam

Great Howe ⑥
pillar
pillar

Brow Gill

Sadgill P
bridge
Whirl How
tumulus

pipes
kiln ⑦
Stockdale

Longsleddale

the warmth of the wood-burning stove and said that they were part of a group of friends from Shap who look after the cottage. They are volunteers and have managed to get some money from the Mountain Bothy Association to help pay towards the repairs. They referred to themselves as the Mosedale 2000 Club, and meet in the Kings Arms Hotel. They deserve a round of applause for their efforts. This diversion to Mosedale does not cost much in terms of height lost and the bothy is a fine refuge on a cold day.

From here take the path that leads SW, towards the main route from Branstree to Tarn Crag. After 400m, just past a rocky knoll, take a four-wheel drive track diagonally across the hill towards Tarn Crag. When it peters out continue SW to the main path along the fence. Near the top, cross the fence and take a path to the cairn on Tarn Crag (48840/07840 elevation 664m (2178ft)) (4). There is a second pipeline pillar, 60m from the cairn (48790/07810).

From Tarn Crag go NE, back to the main path by the fence. This drops down SE and crosses boggy ground near Greycrag Tarn. As you climb the slope, if you can see the cairn on Harrop Pike, head directly to it; alternatively, follow the fence which makes a 90° turn at the top of the slope to head NE to Harrop Pike (50090/07810, elevation 637m (2090ft)) (5). From here, go SW along the fence and continue to Grey Crag, on Sleddale Fell  (49710/07200, elevation 638m (2093ft)).

Now, the way is back to Sadgill over a 1500ft top. A path heads SW through rocky outcrops to a cairn on Great Howe (48920/06420, elevation 494m (1620ft)) (6). A third pipeline pillar is only 50m from the cairn, but as it is lower down the fell it is hidden from sight (49020/06430). A fourth pillar is a further 300m to the south, just over a wall above Brock Crag (49060/06140).

From here descend, by the left of the crags, to a wall by a stream. Follow the wall to a gap (49100/05720) and continue down to a gate. Above are several attractive waterfalls. Take the main track to the buildings at Stockdale. The reservoir pipeline crosses the track at 'DEEP WATER' warning signs. It crosses Brow Gill and swings back down the hillside to cross again, lower down. A quick inspection shows that the water is carried in three pipes.

A large stone structure is passed and our various suggestions included: a loading platform, a ski-jump and a kiln (7). Walk down to the valley road and turn right. On the far side of the road there is a picnic table by the river, another friendly feature of Longsleddale. Even though it was cold we couldn't refuse this invitation to finish our food and drink. On the way back to Sadgill, less than 1km away, notice a tumulus to the left of the road, marked on the map as Whirl Howe. The only wildlife we saw all day was a solitary raven over Branstree and, appropriately, a wren in Wrengill Quarry.

The Plough Inn is just over a mile from Garnett Bridge, on the A6.

# Walk 22. Helvellyn from Patterdale

**Map:** OL5; map ref. prefix NY

**Distance:** 16.5km (10.5 miles)

**Ascent:** 1050m (3440ft)

**Time:** 7½ hours

**Starting point/parking:** By A592 in Patterdale, a lay-by opposite the White Lion has room for several cars (397158). Just NW of the White Lion, is a fee paying parking area. The lane that leads to Grisedale, on the south side of the bridge over Grisedale Beck, has space for about 12 vehicles (390160).

## General Description

The approach is along the Grisedale valley, followed by an ascent of the east ridge of Nethermost Pike. The route continues over Helvellyn and Swirral Edge to Catstycam and returns down Glenridding. In good conditions the climb up the ridge and along Catstycam are easy scrambles. Much of route is on paths, though parts are on scree and open fells. Mining areas, a dam and the scenic area of Keldas, above Glenridding, are visited. I did this walk at the beginning of March, in perfect weather conditions, with excellent snow above 2000ft; crampons were needed for the east ridge of Nethermost Pike and Catstycam.

## Route

North of Patterdale, turn west along the lane by the south side of Grisedale Bridge (one of the parking areas). Walk along this, up Grisedale with the beck on your right and after 1km a bridge is reached (383156). Don't cross the bridge but carry straight on for a further 2km to Crossing Plantation. (I have seen red squirrels in the woods along here.) 200m after the plantation, a path branches right to a footbridge (362143) (1). If you are interested in investigating the mining area below Eagle Crag cross the bridge, otherwise carry on for 1km to Ruthwaite Lodge.

Over the bridge, a spoil heap indicates the mine area. Above and to

Helvellyn summit

the right of the spoil is a ruined hut with a hearth and a shovel! There is a tunnel to the left of the spoil (35820/14190). This is at the bottom of a worked seam that rises straight up the hillside. I thought this was a lead mining area but I found stones with green marks, indicating the presence of copper as well. From the mine, contour south below crags, one has a cave at its foot, to Ruthwaite Lodge. This is maintained by the Outward Bound Ullswater and has a memorial plaque to Richard Read and Mike Evans of the OBU, who died on an expedition to Mount Cook.

Leave the main path and go west into Ruthwaite Cove. Follow the beck and its right branch for 1km until it peters out. Climb north for 100m to Hard Tarn, quite small and well hidden (34630/13800, elevation 716m (2348ft)). It was frozen when I was there but the sun lit up this corner of the cove, making a lovely scene. Contour back NE for 400m, below crags, to gain the east ridge of Nethermost Pike. Scramble up the ridge to the summit. Normally this is easy but crampons are needed in winter conditions.

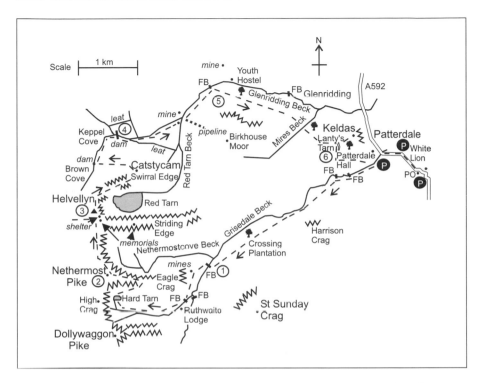

The last part of the ridge is a narrow arête with steep sides, but not quite as spectacular as Striding Edge. At the top of Nethermost Pike, I made the northernmost cairn the highest (34370/14190 elevation 891m (2923ft)) (2).

Take the main path north to Helvellyn, passing two memorials near the top (see Walk 19). The actual summit of Helvellyn, marked by a cairn, is 20m north of a shelter (34240/15100 elevation 950m (3118ft)) (3).

I made a diversion to Striding Edge to photograph the Dixon memorial on Striding Edge mentioned in Walk 19. (On that occasion I had joined Striding Edge just past the memorial). As I dropped down to the ridge, I chatted to another walker who explained that he climbs Helvellyn most days to report on the weather conditions. (The name of the website is *weatherline* – www.lake-distict.gov.uk/weatherline.) His name is Pete Collins and the dog, Drizzi, that accompanied him, is a search and rescue dog. Drizzi was remarkably sure-footed and shot up the awkward little chimney near the west end of the ridge. Recently Pete featured in David Dimbleby's *History of Britain* programme; he is also a member of Patterdale Mountain Rescue Team. A year earlier, I had met members of the Buxton Mountain Rescue team in snow on Striding Edge.

Go past the trig point to a cairn marking the start of the Swirral Edge (34130/15270). Continue along the arête to Catstycam (34800/15820, elevation 890m (2919ft)). From the cairn descend the NW ridge. (The snow was perfect for crampons and made the descent very enjoyable.) Drop down into Brown Cove, to a small pool and old dam (343160). Follow the stream down into Keppel Cove. There is a water leat to the north of the beck. The old dam wall is an impressive construction and looks in reasonable condition considering its age, although a sign says that it is dangerous to walk on (346163) (4). The original dam burst in 1927 causing a great deal of damage though no one was killed. It was rebuilt, but breached again in 1931.

Walk along the south bank of Glenridding Beck. Below, and to the south of the dam, a reedy channel is visible; this disused leat goes for over a kilometre to the top of what was once a pipeline. The line of the leat may be seen on the distant fellside and is marked on OS maps. (It is clearly seen to the east of the path to Red Tarn.) After about 500m, a path leads down to a mine spoil heap with an open tunnel (35640/16680). By the confluence of Glenridding Beck with Red Tarn Beck, the path joins a track, and above are the supports of the pipeline mentioned earlier. Take the track to a footbridge opposite the Greenside Mine area (36290/17310) (5).

Lead was the main ore but silver was also extracted. A chimney flue, one mile long and marked on maps, was built above a smelter near Lucy Tongue Gill. A large silver ingot was lost in a flood in the gill and there is no record of it ever being recovered.

Don't cross the footbridge but stay on the track as it passes above a Youth Hostel and other buildings. This mine track is buttressed and in places rock has been hewn out of the hillside. It is in good condition for 1.5km, until past a footbridge. Continue on the track, ignoring paths that drop down towards Glenridding. Maintain height above the woods at Miresbeck, passing knolls that are excellent viewpoints. Below one of these knolls, 300m after crossing Mires Beck, there is a stile over a wall (38180/16320). Cross it and take a path to Lanty's Tarn. (It was dammed to provide ice for Patterdale Hall.) One theory is that it got its name from the illegal whisky distiller Lanty Slee, but according to A. H. Griffin it's from one Lancelot Dobson, who lived in the area. It was a favourite tarn of Harry Griffin's and he named a house after it (Source: *The Guardian, A Country Diary*). Go past the northern side of the tarn to Keldas for lovely views of Ullswater and an opportunity for photography (6).

From Keldas, return to the western side of Lanty's Tarn. Follow the path south, down to a wall. Turn left and walk to a farm; go right, through the farm buildings, followed by left to a gate at the end of the buildings (385160). Here, go right and drop down to the Patterdale Hall road. Turn right and this leads to the lane by Grisedale Bridge. The White Lion is a good pub for a drink at the end of the walk.

### Note:

1km north of Patterdale, opposite the boating area, there is a stone recess with the name St Patrick's Well (in the wall on the west side of the road). It is said that St Patrick walked from the coast to this area, hence the name Patterdale. Until recently, the name of the inn at Bampton was St Patrick's Well Inn.

# Walk 23. The Dodds from Matterdale

**Map:** OL5; map ref. prefix NY

**Distance:** 17.5km (11 miles)

**Ascent:** 800m (2620ft)

**Time:** 7 hours

**Starting point/parking:** Take the A5091 between Ullswater and the A66. A minor road, New Road, runs west from Dockray. There is space for several cars by a bend near High Row, 1.5km from Dockray (379219).

## General Description

The route starts along the Old Coach Road towards Clough Head. Calfhow Pike, Great Dodd, Watson's Dodd, Stybarrow Dodd and Birkett Fell are visited. The return is past the lovely setting of Dowthwaitehead. Most of the walk is on good paths. Two sections are across open moor. Overall the terrain is relatively gentle.

Jan and I did this walk in January on a day when there was considerable snow on the tops, with a strong, bitterly cold wind.

## The Route

Go through the gate to the west of the car park. The track is named the Old Coach Road and goes round the north of the hill range to St John's in the Vale. There is some doubt as to whether it was ever used by coaches. (Along here we saw a kestrel hovering above the fells.) The track turns to the north at a small footbridge (373222). A path leading over Randerside to Great Dodd branches off west at this point. Keep on the Old Coach Road for a further 3km, past Wolf Crags to a footbridge, Mariel Bridge, over Mosedale Beck (350227) (1).

Over the Mariel Bridge, walk 200m to a bend in the path (34790/22920). Step over the fence and follow a faint path west, aiming for the rocky tor of White Pike. On the way there is an old cabin (34280/22900). From the cabin, go to the edge of the scree that leads up to White Pike; there are good views of Blencathra and Skiddaw. From here, continue up the grassy slope to Clough Head

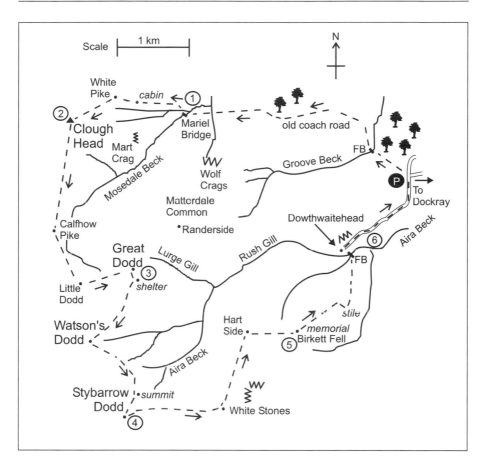

(33390/22550, elevation 726m (2381ft)) (2). In the right conditions you may see paragliders flying in the area.

From Clough Head, follow the main path south for 1.5km to the rocky prominence of Calfhow Pike (33070/21140, elevation 660m (2166ft)). The path goes SE to Little Dodd then swings east, climbing up to Great Dodd (3). Above the snow line, we saw a bird with a white front and a dark line below its neck. It was the right size for a dotterel and I can't think of many species that are likely to be near the top of a mountain in winter conditions. We were hit by a snow squall as we reached the summit cairn ((34200/20560, elevation 857m (2811ft)). We took refuge in the shelter, 150m SE of the cairn. My camera case was blown out of my hands and I chased it down the east side of the

Skiddaw and Blencathra from White Pike

hill. I had no chance of catching it and last saw it spinning across the icy surface towards Lurge Gill.

Take the main path, that starts south and swings SW, for 1km to Watson's Dodd (33560/19560, elevation 789m (2589ft)). Leave the cairn on a good path to Stybarrow Dodd; it starts on a bearing of 110° and swings SE. The main cairn is just to the east of the path (34320/18950, elevation 843m (2766ft)). On a clear day there are excellent views of Thirlmere from a cairn, 300m to the SW (34104/18690) (4). From here, go east, gently downhill for 1km to White Stones (35300/18750, elevation 795m (2608ft)). In winter, you may see skiers using the ski lift, 1km to the south, on Raise. (Whilst skiing along the Dodds I met Bernie who helps to run the ski club. He told me how they skiied in the Millennium using head torches and watched the fireworks of Penrith and Keswick from Raise.)

Follow the ridge northwards for just over 1km to Hart Side (35900/19740, elevation 756m (2481ft)). Then go east for 500m to the cairn on Birkett Fell (36360/19760, elevation 725m (2378ft)) (5). This was named after Lord Birkett whose intervention in the House of Lords debate, 8th Feb 1962, helped stop Manchester from developing Ullswater as a reservoir. The name, Birkett Fell, is chiselled on a piece of rock in the cairn. We took shelter from the cold west wind behind a wall to the east.

One option from here is to go SE and then NE along the ridge over Watermillock Common to Dockray. However, we chose to go NE from Birkett Fell, dropping steeply, off-path but over easy ground to Dowthwaitehead. A fence is met above the farmland and is crossed by a stile (372203). Climb over this and angle down, past a ruined wall, towards the white farmhouse (6).

Cross a footbridge, over Aira Beck, to the farm and walk along the valley road for 1.5km back to the car park. This valley is quite spectacular and one of the remoter spots in the Lakes. Wainwright describes it as a desolate area and one to avoid, but for once I have to disagree with the great man, or perhaps it has changed since those days. The crags surrounding the head of the valley are steep and the streams provide fine waterfalls after heavy rain. Aira Beck flows down to Ullswater resulting in the famous Aira Force Falls below Gowbarrow Fell.

The Royal Hotel at nearby Dockray has a public bar that serves real ales.

### Notes:

If there is time, a visit to Aira Force will complete the day. There is a free car park 800m above Ullswater on the Dockray road (397211). The main waterfall is about 300m from this car park. A bridge above the fall has a memorial to Stephen Edward Spring Rice (1856-1902) and his brother Gerald. The bridge below the fall commemorates Cecil Spring Rice, died 1919, who was an ambassador to the United States. On one visit I saw a dipper just below this bridge.

Also, Wordsworth Point is on the shore of Ullswater, 1.5km SW along the road to Patterdale (389191). This spot is thought to be the inspiration for 'Daffodils'. Other poems about this area by William Wordsworth are 'The Somnambulist', 'The Waterfall and the Eglantine' and 'Airey-Force Valley'.

# Walk 24. The Shap Fells from Wet Sleddale

**Maps:** OL5, OL7; map ref. prefix NY

**Distance:** 20.5km (13 miles)

**Ascent:** 700m (2300ft)

**Time:** 7¾ hours

**Starting point/parking:** From the A6, near the M6 Shap junction, take the road to Wet Sleddale Reservoir. Car park by dam (554113).

## General Description

On the hills a few years ago, I found a 1:25 000 map with crosses marking all the 1500ft tops of the Shap Fells. Eventually I planned this walk from Wet Sleddale, linking many of these hills.

The terrain resembles the Dark Peak District rather than the Lake District and is certainly off the beaten path. Navigation in cloud isn't easy; bogs and tussocks make fast progress difficult but the occasional path does give a little relief. On our trip, Tony and I saw deer, grouse, kestrels and an owl.

## Route

After admiring Wet Sleddale Reservoir, go south out of the car park along an ill-defined track, with grouse butts on the left, to a wall. After 1km, where the track forks, go right, by Howe Gill, for 0.5km to a shooting cabin, the Lunch House (545100) (1). Here, the clouds closed in, the rain started (it lasted for most of the day) and Tony already had problems with his boots. Follow the line of Howe Gill, over rough ground for 1km to visit a large boulder, 200m from the gill, named Gray Bull (53959/09200). From here, walk 500m on 300° to Sleddale Pike, no cairn, (53540/09440, elevation 506m (1659ft)). (We saw deer in this area.)

Go southwards for 1km, to a few stones that mark the summit of Wasdale Pike (53690/08500, elevation 565m (1852ft)). Contour westwards for 1km, crossing a fence, to the various peaks around Great Saddle Crag. We had fun, in thick cloud, trying to determine the high-

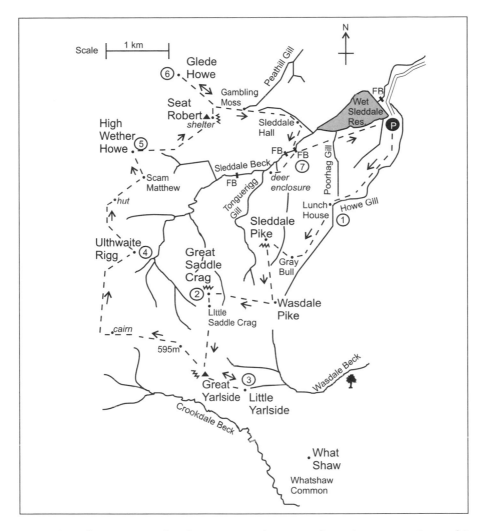

est point; this appeared to be at 52620/08660, elevation 564m (1850ft) (2). Go south over Little Saddle Crag (52700/08300, elevation 572m (1877ft)). (Near here, we disturbed a short-eared owl and several grouse.)

Continue south to Great Yarlside; the going becomes easier on the higher ground. There is a 'bubble' trig point, set in a concrete surround, 5m from the wall, on the far side (52550/07590). Go SE along a path (a bonus!) by the wall to Little Yarlside. The highest point is on the north side of the wall (53200/07170, elevation 516m (1691ft)) (3). Here, when the clouds lifted for a few minutes, we were rewarded by a view of the surrounding fells.

In 1975 an American fighter, an F-111, crashed near the top. There is a crater, 15m from the wall, that may have been caused by the crash, but I didn't find any wreckage (53258/07060).

Walk back to Great Yarlside and continue along the wall. Another high point on the ridge, south of Brown Howe, is unnamed (52090/07920, elevation 595m (1952ft)). The next target is Ulthwaite Rigg. Rather than a direct, off-path route, we chose the luxury of the path along the fence for 1km, past a cairn, to a fence junction (50950/08000). On old 1 inch:1 mile maps there is a spot height at this cairn of 1963ft. Go north for 1km, by the side of a fence, then contour, bearing 060°, to Ulthwaite Rigg (51460/09350, elevation 502m (1648ft)) (4). The terrain can only be described as atrocious. From this spot we had a fleeting (and tempting) glimpse of Wet Sleddale Reservoir.

Head NW across more, lovely ground back to the fence. Follow this north to a track (51030/09970). Near here, we saw the carcass of a young deer whose hind leg had been caught in the fence wire. Westwards along Mosedale, the bothy of Mosedale Cottage looked tantalisingly close. Turn right and go 700m along the track passing a cabin that appears to have formerly been the back of a truck (51190/10100). It's firmly strapped to the ground but the means of access was beyond our technical skills. Climb up the little peak of Scam Matthew and head northwards to the cairn on High Wether Howe (51490/10920, elevation 531m (1742ft)) (5).

Near the cairn is a fence that goes east and there is a track just to the north of it. Take this towards Seat Robert, which is just over 1km away, on a bearing of 060°. A fine cairn and shelter mark the summit of Seat Robert so there should be no chance of a mistake (52640/11410, elevation 515m (1688ft)).

The last peak to be 'bagged' is Glede Howe. By visiting this before Seat Robert a little distance could be saved but it would involve crossing a valley and awkward terrain (if by this stage you still care). Go north for 200m, then NW, keeping to the high ground. The first peak, 800m from Seat Roberts, is Glede Howe (52120/12040, elevation

Sleddale Beck Bridge

476m (1562ft)) (6). Surprisingly, it is higher than the more prominent peak and cairn 200m further on. Return towards Seat Robert and pass below its north side. A track is picked up that can be followed to the wall over Gambling Moss (52680/11560). We dropped below the clouds and had good views of Wet Sleddale Reservoir. Follow the wall to a stile in a corner (53810/11590). Over the stile, follow a wall down to Sleddale Hall. Sadly, the condition of the buildings is deteriorating. Drop down further to the barn and take the track by a wall, bearing 190°. At the bottom, go over a stile (white arrow) to Sleddale Bridge, built when the reservoir was created (7).

After crossing the bridge, there is an opportunity to visit a complex of walls that once formed a deer enclosure (537106). This is 500m to the west, through two gates. The walls, seven feet high in places were originally quite a bit higher. From the bridge, a path goes east, on the south side of the reservoir, back to the car park.

If you have visited all the tops you will have collected nine 1500ft tops and got very wet feet; blame the person who lost that map. In the unlikely event that you see anyone else walking these fells, I would steer well clear of them – they're probably insane.

After getting out of our wet gear we visited the Greyhound Hotel, 1 mile along the A6 towards Shap, enjoyed a fine pint of Hartley's and admired the size of the blister on one of Tony's heels.

### Notes:

Sleddale Hall featured in the 1987 film 'Withnail and I'. It was Uncle Monty's cottage, Crow Cragg. The bridge is where Withnail shoots fish with a shotgun.

As you drive along the A6 to Shap Village, you may see boulders in a far corner of a field. This stone circle is on your right, nearly opposite the cement works.

Also, in Shap, there is a memorial plaque to two pilots of RAF 100 Squadron who died in a crash close to the village on 22 October 1999. The plaque is on the bridge to the north of the village, on the east side of the road.

# Walk 25. A Martindale Horseshoe

**Map:** OL5; map ref. prefix NY

**Distance:** 21.5km (13.5 miles); (19km, 12 miles if The Nab is omitted)

**Ascent:** 1390m (4560ft)

**Time:** 9¼ hours

**Starting point/parking:** Take the road to Howtown off the B5320 near Pooley Bridge. At the Church of St Martin, near Christy Bridge, there is space for a few cars (434184). Alternatively park opposite the Church of St Peter (435192). **Note:** Parts of the deer conservation area, around The Nab, may be closed Sept – Feb.

## General Description

This walk goes over Beda Fell to Angle Tarn, Rest Dodd and Rampsgill Head. It returns along the northern part of High Street. It is on excellent paths apart from a couple of short sections. An aircraft wreck site is near the route. Deer are likely to be seen near The Nab. Two lovely old churches may be visited and in the valley there is a hunting lodge where the Kaiser once stayed. When I did this walk in May it was warm and sunny.

## Route

From the old church of St Martin, walk SW along the road and over Christy Bridge. Directly past the farm, take the footpath on the right that climbs diagonally beneath Winter Crag. Don't take the path marked 'Bridleway to Sandwick', the path required goes past the arrow indicating the bridleway. After 400m the ridge leading south to Beda Head is reached and an iron seat gives lovely views towards Sandwick (1). Walk along the ridge, on a good path. Above Low Brock Crags, a few metres to the west of the path, is a small stone shelter (428173). I saw a buzzard in the valley to the east and skylarks were singing overhead as I reached Beda Head (42800/17050, elevation 509m (1670ft)).

A Lockheed Hudson crashed near the summit in 1942, killing all four crew. A very small amount of wreckage remains. To find it, carry

The view from Angletarn Pikes

on south for 150m to a rise. Look for a small pool of water, 100m to the west. The wreckage is 10m from the pool on its east side (42700/17086).

The ridge dips, then rises to Beda Fell and passes over knolls to a cairn on Bedafell Knott (42000/15970). Continue along the ridge to another cairn. Here, I met a walker, Reg Alexander, who was making good progress despite having serious problems with both knees. We chatted about how quiet and lovely the area was, also about 'The Bungalow' (see later). Before Angletarn Pikes there is a cairnless, grassy knoll (41540/14980). From here, go SW to the first Angletarn Pike (41330/14820 elevation 567m (1860ft)). The small crag provides a scramble right of centre. Go to the other pike, 200m to the SE (41430/14700, elevation 565m (1854ft)) (2). This is a good viewpoint for Angle Tarn. Having seen only one walker so far, it came as a surprise to see several large groups. There is another cairnless knoll, worth visiting for views of Bannerdale, 500m to the NE across boggy ground, above Heck Cove (41830/14950).

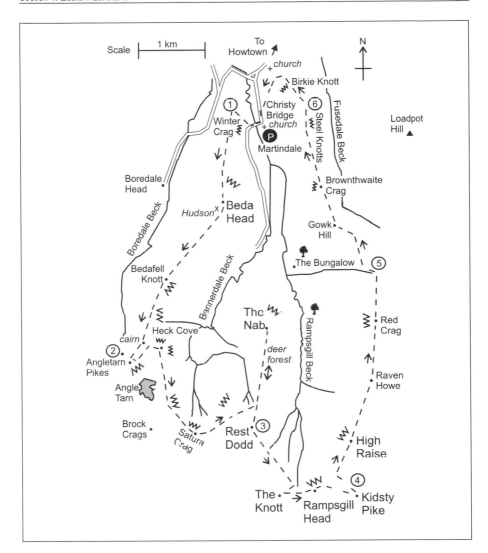

From here go south, then SE round the head of Bannerdale, over another minor rise, to Satura Crag. Keep near the edge, the main path is close by but doesn't give the best views. From Satura Crag, go eastwards on a thin path towards Rest Dodd.

If you feel energetic and have an hour to spare, a visit to The Nab is a possibility. For this, take a left fork (42470/13640). Go to a stile in a wall, cross it and follow the wall as it swings to the ridge leading to

The Nab. (I saw a few deer below here but at certain times of the year this may be closed because it is a deer conservation area.) Drop down to the ridge and go north across marshy ground to the summit cairn of The Nab (43430/15200, elevation 576m (1890ft)). Return south and climb steeply to Rest Dodd. The eastern cairn is the highest (43270/13700, elevation 696m (2283ft)) (3).

Descend, on a bearing of 150°, to the col between Rest Dodd and The Knott. Years ago, by the wall below the summit, I saw an elderly gentleman with white hair, smoking a pipe and writing or sketching on a note pad. Apart from the two of us, the area was totally deserted but as I passed close by him, contrary to the usual courtesy, he didn't acknowledge my presence. I wondered if it could have been A.W. himself!

The slog along the main path, by the wall, up to The Knott is tedious. It is better to keep to the north, above the head of the Ramps Gill valley, and ascend on grass, with excellent views along the valley. As you near The Knott, contour round to the cairn on the far side of the wall (43710/12690, elevation 739m (2423ft)). Climb diagonally eastwards for 500m to the summit of Rampsgill Head (44220/12770 elevation 792m (2598ft)).

A quick visit to Kidsty Pike gives views along Riggindale. It is only 500m to the east, across grassy land, to the summit (44740/12600 elevation 780m (2560ft)) (4).

From Kidsty Pike a path heads 340° to join the main path to the cairn and shelter on High Raise (44820/13450, elevation 802m (2632ft)). Keep walking northwards, by the fence, on a good path over Raven Howe and Red Crag. This is part of the old Roman road (High Street). 400m after Red Crag leave this path, and go through a gate in the wall that goes down by the side of Mere Beck (452160) (5). Cross to the north side of a dry gully and take the path downhill, by the wall for 300m. Stay on the path for a further 500m as it swings northwards and then leave it to make the short climb up Gowk Hill (44470/16700, elevation 470m (1542ft)).

At the bottom of Mere Beck is a building with a red roof, known as The Bungalow. It was built in 1910 by the Earl of Lonsdale, as a deer-hunting lodge for a visit by Kaiser Wilhelm. In World War Two it was used as an officers' mess by the army who trained in the area. Reg, whom I had met earlier, explained that it now belonged to the Dalemain Estate and could be rented as a holiday cottage.

From Gowk Hill, drop down NE to a path near a wall leading to Brownthwaite Crag (44300/17360). On the far side of the crag, follow the path to a low point on the ridge. A path slants down the hillside back to the old church and the start of the walk. However, we go over a stile and climb northwards to Steel Knotts, which starts with a rocky outcrop (44037/18124). Continue along the ridge to a cairn and views of Ullswater (43950/18600) (6). Leave the path along the ridge and descend to the left. When St Peter's Church comes in view head directly towards it, keeping the crags of Birkie Knott on your left. The grassy slope is steep and a test for tired knees. At the bottom by a concrete GPO post, a path that passes behind the church is reached. Turn left and follow the path below crags. Look for a gate, on the right, in a corner of the wall. Go through this and walk round to a seat at a lovely viewpoint. The path continues in front of a row of cottages and slants down to the road close to St Martin's Church.

The church has been there since at least 1266 and has an ancient yew tree behind it. The altar table is dated 1674. The font is thought to be Roman and to have come from High Street. St Peter's Church is also very attractive with its red sandstone and beautiful stained glass windows. These have explanations of their scenes printed alongside. Sadly, there was a note saying that the church had been broken into three times in four months. Yet both churches were unlocked, and a visit to them made a perfect finish to my walk. Well not quite the finish: I met Jan, who had walked along the path to Patterdale, by the side of Ullswater, and we caught the boat back. We visited the tiny public bar of the Howtown Hotel and sat in the small garden at the back of the hotel.

# Walk 26. A Haweswater Horseshoe

**Map:** OL5; map ref. prefix NY

**Distance:** 25.5km (16 miles)

**Ascent:** 1270m (4170)

**Time:** 10½ hours (should take less, as much of the walk is on good paths)

**Starting point/parking:** Parking area for several cars at Burnbanks, east end of Haweswater, by a footpath signpost (508161).

## General Description

The idea is to go over the tops of the hills surrounding Haweswater. A clockwise horseshoe means that the awkward part is tackled first. The main problem is gaining the heights to the south of the dam, to get the views from Hugh's Laithes Cairn. Some of the first stage is off-path and over boggy terrain. After this, a route may be followed that is on reasonable tracks or good paths. I first did this walk in the opposite direction, taking in the Measand Valley, with Malc and Brian. On my latest visit, in October, I was alone and it was sunny at the start.

An information board, by the phone-box, gives a brief history of the building of the Haweswater reservoir. The act was passed in 1919 but the dam wasn't completed until 1940 and the reservoir took two years to fill.

## Route

Take the footpath through the wood to Naddle Bridge. Turn right and walk along the road for 300m and at a bend, carry straight on along a right of way to Naddle Farm. (Just past the farm an aqueduct carrying water from Swindale crosses Naddle Beck.) At the farm, the problem is that the right of way turns east to Swindale, while you would prefer to carry on southwards along a track to open access land, 300m away. A nearby water board sign says 'no public access' but Wainwright's Naddle Horseshoe uses this track. I have been this way, there are no gates and I had no problems. If you go this way, at the start of the open access area, (50810/14980), take the path for 300m and then fork right

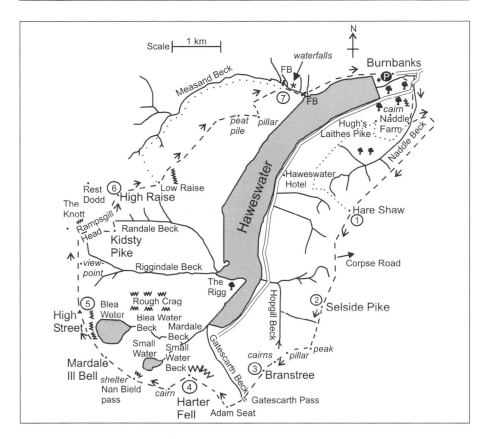

along a track up the hillside. At the end of the track, head NW to a fence and follow it to a new gate (50080/14790).

The alternative route from Naddle Farm uses the sign-posted path to Swindale for 800m to reach open access land (51610/15120). Then turn SW for 2km to the bottom of Powley's Hill, this can be included on the way to Hare Shaw (but the opportunity of visiting Hugh's Laithes Cairn is missed).

(I have climbed up the eastern end of the shoulder above Haweswater, from the path between Naddle Farm and the road along the reservoir. This is the shortest route but the way through the crags isn't open access land; it is also difficult terrain and there is a deer fence near the top (there is a gate at 50710/15320).)

If you take the track south from Naddle Farm, from the gate, (50080/14790), go 350m on a bearing of 020° to Hugh's Laithes Cairn, for good views of the Haweswater Dam. (I saw two deer on my way to the cairn.) Unfortunately the cairn is on the other side of a deer fence. Some pieces of wood had been placed to facilitate the climb over it. Climb back over the fence and go 600m on 250° to another cairn. Go through a gate in the nearby wall and continue for 1.5km over small rises to a gate in another wall (48970/13730). The going underfoot is still difficult but some patches are better than others. Go east along the wall to a new gate and then SE, still off-path but over ground that begins to improve, to a cairn on Hare Shaw (49740/13120) (1).

Take a track, made by vehicles, towards Selside Pike on a bearing of about 200°.

On the way, the Old Corpse Road from Mardale to Swindale is crossed, marked by a stake (49490/12300). A good path rises to the shelter at Selside Pike (49070/11170, elevation 655m (2149ft)) (2). Follow the fence downhill and then step over it to climb a nameless bump to the south. Drop down this to a survey pillar (48370/10260), (For more details of the pipeline pillars see Walk 21). Walk up to the two fine cairns on Artle Crag and head back towards the fence, near the summit of Branstree with its circular trig point (47800/09960, elevation 713m (2339ft)) (3). Somewhere in this region a scene from the film *Withnail and I*, showing Haweswater, was shot (see Walk 24).

The walk, all the way from here to High Raise is on well-used paths. Not far from Branstree summit, by the fence on the way down to Gatescarth Pass, is an old boundary stone bearing the letter L. Cross the boggy dip and go over Adam Seat and Little Harter Fell, a good viewpoint for Haweswater. On the way up Harter Fell a cairn with oddly shaped iron posts is passed. In cloud, people sometimes mistake this for the summit. Just past here is another boundary marker, this time bearing the letter H. Continue along the fence to the summit (45970/09320, elevation 778m (2552ft)) (4). In poor visibility, take care heading down to Nan Bield Pass. The start of the descent is marked by a cairn 130m from the summit, on a bearing of 260°.

A tarn, Small Water, lies to the north and has some tiny shelters close to it. To the south are views of Kentmere Reservoir, a 150 year-old artificial lake. Along here, I chatted with a gentleman, Tony from Grasmere, who recommended the novel *Haweswater* by Sarah Hall. After a quick bite to eat and some more conversation in the shelter at Nan Bield Pass, I bid farewell and, in a heavy shower, headed up the path to Mardale Ill Bell (44760/10110, elevation 760m (2493ft)).

SELSIDE PIKE    BRANSTREE    HARTER FELL

ROUGH CRAG

The view along Riggindale

The main path swings northwards to the trig point on High Street (44089/11050, elevation 828m (2717ft)) (5). A point 80m to the north seems higher, but this is of little consequence. A crag juts out over Riggindale giving views along this desolate valley, where the Lakeland's eagle(s) live. A small tarn on the ridge over Rough Crag is visible. Once, along this ridge, an eagle flew close to me, just below the top of the crags.

Continuing north along the wall take the right fork towards Kidsty Pike (43930/12250). On the way to the Pike, make a diversion to Rampsgill Head for the views to the north (44220/12770, elevation 792m (2598ft)). Cut across eastwards to the cairn at Kidsty Pike (44740/12600 elevation 780m (2560ft)). Head 340°, to pick up the main path to the cairn and shelter on High Raise (44820/13450, elevation 802m (2632ft)) (6). Head 070° along a path to Low Raise, which also has a low shelter (45650/13770, elevation 754m (2474ft)).

The easiest way from here is to continue along the top of the wide ridge that heads to the right of north from Low Raise. A pleasant track, starting NE, made by four-wheel drive vehicles goes all the way along the moor. The Southern Strollers, Jan, Marilyn, Robert and Jake used this route earlier in the summer, whilst on the Coast to Coast Walk and they enthused over it (I was support driver/guide for this fine crew!).

A masochistic, squelchy alternative is to drop down NW from Low Raise, into the valley below. On my previous horseshoe walk we started by walking up this valley. It certainly is remote; it is also extremely boggy with no real paths, though we did see deer, fell ponies and a large bird of prey. The valley route curves round, along Measand Beck to Haweswater.

The way on the top of the moor leads to a grass-covered peat stack that may be seen from some distance away (46580/14830). Near the end of the ridge, just before the path drops steeply into the valley, walk towards the eastern edge for views of Haweswater. An old survey pillar stands here and it appears to be in line with the pillars on the far side that mark the pipeline along Longsleddale (47600/15100). Go down Measand End to a footbridge over Measand Beck (7). Stay on the south side and keep close to the beck for the best views of the waterfalls. A narrow gorge is followed by falls where the water shoots out at several places. At the bottom, go over a footbridge and along the track back to Burnbanks.

There is an inn, at Bampton, where I have stayed several times. It has recently changed its name from the St Patrick's Well Inn to the Mardale Inn. Alternatively, there is the Crown and Mitre Hotel at Bampton Grange: when our Coast to Coast team visited here, the landlord kindly gave Jake a bowl of water and something to eat.

### Note:

The latest information regarding the Mardale eagles, is that the old female, having been in the valley for 28 years and raising nine young, is now assumed dead as she has not been sighted since 2004. However, a young male has been in residence since 2002 and there is hope that he might find a partner (November 2005). There is a hide in Riggindale that is manned from late March to the end of August. When I was there a few years ago a telescope gave clear views of the nest.

*Opposite: Loweswater (Walk 27)*

# Section 5: Western Lakeland

# Walk 27. Blake Fell and Hen Comb from Loweswater

**Map:** OL4; map ref. prefix NY

**Distance:** 18km (11 miles) (Including Hen Comb and Mellbreak)

**Ascent:** 1310m (4300ft) (Including Hen Comb and Mellbreak)

**Time:** 8 hours

**Starting point/parking:** From the road SE of Loweswater (Lake), take the lane to Maggie's Bridge to a free NT car park (134210).

## General Description

This walk takes in the fells to the west of Loweswater and Crummock Water. Hen Comb and Mellbreak may be included. It is mainly on grassy paths but some stretches are likely to be boggy. In September, I saw several red squirrels near Loweswater. Despite warning signs (to drivers not squirrels), one of them had been run over.

## Route

Take the track towards Watergate Farm and, 50m before it take the path on the right to Loweswater. Go through a gate and immediately turn left up a path that rises diagonally through Holme Wood. Cross two tracks and turn right, slightly downhill along the third (12270/21160). This leads to the waterfalls of Holme Beck. Climb up a path on the left side of a waterfall, Holme Force. Continue upwards, passing one point where the pressure forces water upwards in a spout, to the top of the waterfalls. The path becomes less defined as it goes up steeply and then through bracken to a wall. To avoid climbing this, go right, to the beck, and carefully round the end of the wall.

Follow the beck for 300m and go over a stile. Cross the beck to the north side and go up a gap in the bracken, by the side of scree. Climb up alongside the fence on the right, with views of Loweswater below. Just over the crest is a cairn (11440/21380) (1). Take a path that leads SW to the summit of Burnbank Fell, on the far side of a fence (11000/20950, elevation 475m (1558ft)). (Here, I was attacked by flying ants.)

Go south along the fence for 500m, then head, on 100°, to Carling Knott. A well-built shelter, just large enough for three or four very close friends, marks the summit (11720/20320, elevation 544m (1785ft)) (2). Continue NE for 500m to a cairn at the end of the ridge for views to the east, and then return to the shelter.

Take a path westwards towards Blake Fell but, as it starts to rise, branch right towards the fence line (11230/20030). Cross the fence and go east, over awkward ground to Sharp Knott (10700/20100, elevation 482m (1581ft)). There is a sunken shelter 30m further to the west and views of Cogra Moss Reservoir and the coast.

Follow a good path SE to Blake Fell (11040/19670, elevation 573m (1880ft)) (3).

At the cairn I met my first people of the day, a group who had come up from the west. At a mention of Loweswater one man waxed lyrically about the Kirkstile Inn. Head southwards by the fence and then follow the ridge and fence that swing west to High Pen. No cairn marks the summit (approx. 11000/18890, elevation 475m (1558ft)).

Cross the fence and find a path that goes east to the col below Gavel Fell. Follow the path alongside the fence to the summit (11700/18370, elevation 526m (1726ft)) (4).

If you wish to return to Maggie's Bridge there is a good track, 750m to the east that leads directly back. Otherwise continue southwards, by the fence, and over a dip to Banna Fell. Leave the fence at the crest and go to the summit, no cairn (approx. 11580/17410, elevation 456m (1496ft)).

Return to the fence and head east, alongside another fence, to the shapely peak of Floutern Cop. Continue eastwards to join a path to a circle of stones marked 'Cairn' on OS maps (12720/17460). This ancient ring of stones is 5m in diameter with a pit in the centre. The path continues to a fence below Hen Comb. Cross this, go left for 50m and climb the slope to a path, (13010/17670), that leads to the cairn on Hen Comb (13220/18120, elevation 509m (1670ft)) (5). (Once more, I was assailed by flying ants at the summit.)

The sensible, pleasant route is to go north along the ridge, over Little Dodd, turn east down to stepping-stones over Mosedale Beck and join the track to Loweswater. However, due to a chance meeting I wanted to include Mellbreak in my round of the fells. Some years ago,

The view from Mellbreak

on the Scottish Southern Upland Walk, I met two sisters Dorene and Joan Parr. Dorene and her husband had moved from the Lake District to Dunnet Head, the most northerly point of Scotland, and they named their new house after their favourite hill but with the Scottish spelling 'Melbreck', meaning 'hollow in the hill'.

To include it on your round, drop down the steep slope on a bearing of 110°. Low down, try to find the shortest way through bracken. Cross Mosedale Beck (13820/17850). Go eastwards on a sheep path (14170/17750), through tussocky grass, to a gate on a north/south track (14360/17900). (There is just a gate; no wall or fence survives.) The sheep path continues on the other side of the track and heads uphill through the bracken (a bonus!). Climb up, steeply, to the rocky, southern end of Mellbreak where the reward is views of Crummock Water and Buttermere. Join the main path to the southern top (14840/18620, elevation 512m (1678ft)). Follow the ridge north, over a dip, to the northern top (14320/19480, elevation 509m (1670ft)) (6).

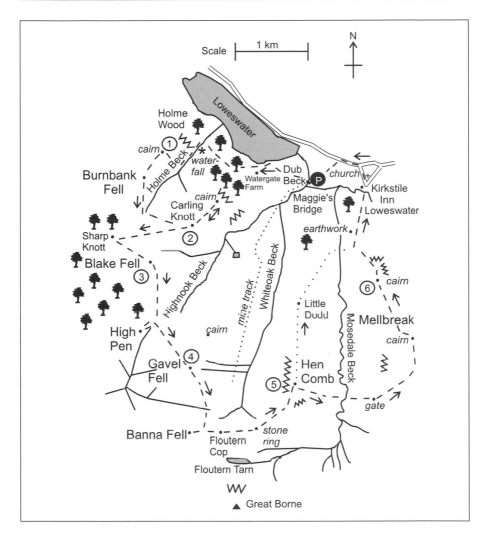

Scale |—— 1 km ——|

N

Loweswater

Holme
Wood

cairn ①

Holme Beck

water-
fall

*

Dub
Beck

Watergate
Farm

church

Kirkstile
Inn
Loweswater

Burnbank
Fell

cairn

Carling
Knott

②

Maggie's
Bridge

earthwork

Sharp
Knott

Blake Fell

③

Highnook Beck

mine track

Whiteoak Beck

Little
Dudd

cairn ⑥

Mellbreak

cairn

High
Pen

cairn

Mosedale Beck

Gavel
Fell

④

Hen
Comb

⑤

gate

Banna Fell

stone
ring

Floutern
Cop

Floutern Tarn

▲ Great Borne

A path zigzags down the nose of Mellbreak, NW through scree, to a
gate. A track leads to the aforementioned Kirkstile Inn. On the way,
over the wall on the left, by a right angle bend, ancient raised earth-
works may be seen (139203). The Kirkstile Inn brews its own beers,
including: Kirkstyle Gold, Grasmoor Dark and Melbreak Bitter, and
sells them at very reasonable prices.

# Walk 28. High Crag and Red Pike from Buttermere

**Map:** OL4; map ref. prefix NY

**Distance:** 18km (11 miles)

**Ascent:** 1220m (4000ft)

**Time:** 8 hours

**Starting point/parking:** At the bottom of Newlands Pass near Buttermere (178172); in Buttermere (charge) or at a NT car park just north of Buttermere.

## General Description

This walk takes an unusual route up High Crag. Then, a good path is followed, over Red Pike and on to Great Borne. The next stage is off path to Scale Force, one of the longest waterfalls in the Lake District. Most of the route is on good paths but some of it is across boggy and tussocky ground, and there is one steep section with some scree.

## Route

From the Fish Hotel, take the track to the west tip of Buttermere Lake and the bottom of Sourmilk Gill (incidentally, a fine, Grade 2 scramble). Follow the path for 2km along the SW shore of the lake, through Birkness (Burtness) Wood. Where Comb Beck flows into the lake, by a sign for a bridleway, leave the path and follow the beck up towards Birkness (Burtness) Comb (18410/15310) (1). (Also at the bottom of the beck is a stone seat, a memorial to a young man, Stuart Elliott, from his friends.) There is a faint path, on the north side of the beck, leading to a wall and stile (18050/14920).

Continue into the comb to get good views of the impressive cliffs that surround it (17680/14580). To the right, below High Stile, are Grey Crags with some lower grade climbs and two good, Grade 3 scrambles, Harrow Buttress and Chockstone Ridge. To the left of Grey Crags is Eagle Crag with more serious climbs, including Bill Peascod's Eagle Front (VS).

To the south of Comb Beck is High Crag Buttress. This consists of steep cliffs, but above these a grassy rake makes its way up

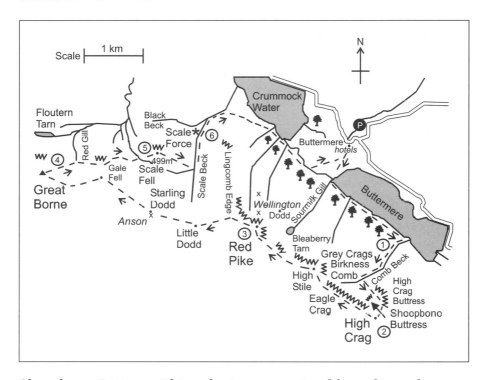

Sheepbone Buttress. This rake is very noticeable and may be seen from Buttermere. Aim directly for it, through a gap in the lower crags (17900/14470). The rake is steep but not difficult. At first keep to the side of the scree below the crag on the right, then use the grass. From the top of the rake there are fine views of Buttermere (18100/14410). Climb the ridge, (I couldn't resist a short scramble up the rocks on the right) to the summit of High Crag (18050/14000, elevation 744m (2442ft)) (2).

Follow a good path, westwards along the edge of the cliffs to High Stile. It is difficult to decide which of several cairns is the highest. I made it to be the one at (16970/14790, elevation 806m (2644ft)), whilst the OS map gives an elevation of 807m (2648ft) at (17010/14810). Continue along the cliff tops to the cairn and shelter at the summit of Red Pike (16050/15450, elevation 755m (2478ft)) (3).

In 1944 a Wellington bomber struck the north facing crags of Red Pike killing all eight Canadian crew. Many small fragments of the aircraft lie on the scree slopes due north of the summit. The highest

The view from High Stile

piece I found was about 50m below (16044/15514). There are bits of wire and aluminium amongst the scree, down to 520m (1700ft), (15987/15803). I have listed more map references at the end of the description.

Take the path along the ridge as it swings NW then turns westwards to Little Dodd, 1km away (14910/15520, elevation 590m(1936ft)). This has a rather artistic sculpture made from metal fence posts. From Little Dodd continue, on the path by a fence, to Starling Dodd. The path leaves the fence after a while then rejoins it just before Starling Dodd. An aircraft, an Anson, crashed near here in 1944. The only wreckage I could find was a small piece of aluminium, which I placed at the bottom of the summit cairn (14210/15740, elevation 633m (2077ft)).

A path descends NW from Starling Dodd and rises slightly, after 1km, to a knoll on Gale Fell (13380/16380). Go round a fenced-off conservation area and continue along the fence to Great Borne. There is a trig point and a shelter to the left of the fence (12390/16370, elevation 616m (2021ft)) (4). Cross the fence to another cairn to the north.

Go east, off-path, dropping down the slope, with a view of Floutern Tarn. I had intended to descend by Red Gill but the fine views persuaded me to maintain height. Walk to the top of Red Gill and contour eastwards above the steep slopes to the north, past a small stone shelter (13570/16490). (Many wheatears and meadow pipits were on the moor.) About 1km from the shelter, on a hill just to the north of east is a boulder that looks like a cairn. To get there head eastwards across the moor, then swing NE over more difficult, heathery terrain. The reddish boulder is near the top of this seldom-visited hill (14340/16810, elevation 499m (1637ft)) (5). There is a small tarn to the west of the boulder and views of Hen Comb and Mellbreak.

Head 110° for 600m, dropping down to Scale Beck. It is possible to walk alongside this pretty beck as far as a waterfall (15020/16900). Then follow the path down to the bottom of Scale Force where a bridge gives a view of the falls (6). An easy scramble to the left of the nearest waterfall, under a holly bush, leads to the foot of the main fall. This is a better place to appreciate this narrow gorge and the main waterfall.

From the bridge follow the path east, to the lake and back to Buttermere. Here, I met Jan who had walked round the lake. We saw a redstart on our way to the Bridge Hotel where we enjoyed the Black Sheep bitter.

### Note:

More map refs of Wellington wreckage: 16003/15756, 16006/15690, 15970/15642, 16223/15593, 16029/15554, 16037/15530.

# Walk 29. Pillar and Steeple from Honister Pass

**Map:** OL4; map ref. prefix NY

**Distance:** 19km (12 miles)

**Ascent:** 1660m (5500ft)

**Time:** 9 hours

**Starting point/parking:** At the top of Honister Pass the NT car park is free to members (225135). The neighbouring slate quarry makes a reasonable charge. A large parking area is 10 minutes walk down the east side of the pass.

## General Description

Ennerdale isn't an easy valley to reach. The track from the lake is rather dull (a mountain bike is one solution or another, as an old Ward Lock guidebook suggests, is rowing! In those days the Anglers' Hotel (Inn), by the NW shore of the lake, would have made the perfect finish to the day). Honister Pass is my alternative start, with the quarries and mines providing interest. The route goes from the top of the Pass, drops down into Ennerdale and up Black Sail Pass. The High Level Traverse is taken to Pillar Rock. Pillar and Steeple are visited. Ennerdale is recrossed on the way to Haystacks and a disused mine tramway provides an easy finish. Nearly all the route is on paths, but in ice or snow the High Level Traverse should be avoided.

## Route

From the quarry buildings, walk westwards up the quarry road. En route, two stone plaques with inscriptions that are worth reading are passed. Take the left fork at a junction (21820/13740). Before upright stones that mark the line of the road, turn left and go to the site of the drum house (21590/13470) (1). This is at the highest part of the old tramway. The drum house contained the winding gear to haul and lower the slate. Continue south on a good path, take the right fork and contour above the hollow of Dubs Bottom (21360/12630). Continue to Loft Beck and descend, steps in places, to the Ennerdale Valley, a loss of 300m (1000ft) in height. Turn right to a footbridge, 300m SE of Black Sail Youth Hostel.

Cross the bridge and climb the path by Sail Beck to the top of Black Sail Pass (2). Take the path NW to Looking Stead. A cairn marks the start of the High Level Traverse (18400/11670, elevation 640m). Along this airy path are fine views of the valley, the afforestation below and the crags above. After 1km, at Robinson's Cairn, Pillar Rock is in sight. Below the cairn is a memorial to John Robinson of Lorton, who died in 1907. Inscribed are these words:

> "We climb the hill: from end to end
> of all the landscape underneath,
> we find no place that does not breathe
> some gracious memory of our friend"

Continue towards Pillar Rock. It is possible to explore round the base of the rock along a climbers' path, Green Ledge. A notice, saying the Mountain Rescue kit has been removed to Gillerthwaite, is passed. A mossy gully, Waterfall Gully, on the west side of the ledge is reached. Don't go any further and return to the east side of Pillar Rock.

Ascend to a point opposite the top of Pillar Rock by climbing scree to the bottom of a path (17320/12220). This is at the edge of the crag, named Shamrock, to the east of Pillar Rock. This path, the Shamrock Traverse, leads steeply and exposed in places, to the southern base of Pisgah, the pinnacle opposite High Man. The cleft between the two is called Jordan Gap. Walker's Gully, named after a man who died in a fall there, is below, between Pillar Rock and Shamrock.

It is possible to scramble down, to the west of Pisgah, to see the various climbs on the west face of Pillar Rock. My climbing experience here is limited. I even managed to go wrong on the New West route, a popular V Diff, when I forgot to step out of the final chimney and continued up the narrowing crack. At one point I had to pull my feet up with my hands – most undignified! The easiest way up High Man is the 'Slab and Notch', a Grade 3 scramble. From the path you may see people on this. I came here in April with Tony L. to try to complete his Lakes 2000'ers but there was so much snow that we couldn't even risk the High Level Traverse. (I have seen a ring ouzel near Pillar Rock.)

HIGH
MAN
PISGAH
LOW
MAN
SHAMROCK
TRAVERSE

Pillar Rock from Robinson's Cairn

Continue up the path to the summit of Pillar (17120/12100 elevation 892m (2927ft)) (3). Go SW from the cairn, down to Wind Gap and climb up to Black Crag (16560/11650, elevation 828m (2717ft)). Continue westwards to Scoat Fell; the summit cairn is on the wall (15940/11390, elevation 841m (2760ft)). (The OS map differentiates between Little Scoat Fell and Great Scoat Fell. Most people consider these to be one hill, with the highest point being where Little Scoat Fell is placed on the map. Great Scoat Fell is marked as being lower and 500m to the west.) Go westwards, swing north and scramble to the top of Steeple (15750/11670, elevation 819m (2687ft)) (4). Notice wild Mirk Cove to the east and Mirklin Cove to the west (OS name is Mirkiln Cove).

Descend northwards along the ridge. Before it turns NW, at 15460/12200, drop NE down the grassy slope, on the left of scree, to the top of the forest by High Beck. Go down the path on the west side of the beck to a gate/stile and enter the trees. By forest standards the path isn't too bad, just the usual tree roots and mossy stones; I

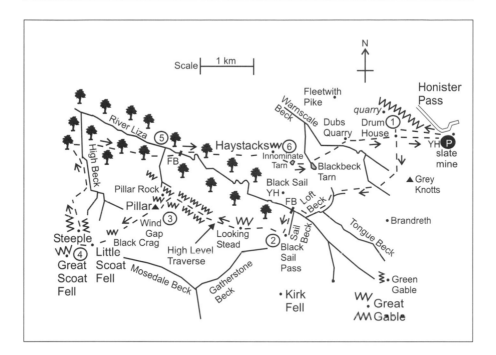

managed one spectacular tumble and about 30 stumbles. The path leads to a forest road (15550/13300). Turn right and walk, uphill for the first 300m, along this easy track. From a bridge the potential of High Beck may be appreciated. Hopefully, one day it will be liberated from the forest surrounding it. Further on, Pillar Rock appears dramatically above, resembling an alpine peak. The road leads to a footbridge over the River Liza (5).

The Fell and Rock Climbing Club contributed to the cost of building the bridge, as a memorial to their members who died in World War Two. A plaque on the far side commemorates this.

Cross the bridge and go up to the main valley track. Turn right for 100m to where a path branches left (17710/13220). Take this, climbing diagonally through a graveyard of trees and over scree. Height is gained steadily, several stiles are climbed and you arrive at the main path to Scarth Gap. Go up to the Gap, turn right and climb to the summit of Haystacks (19300/13240, elevation 597m (1959ft)) (6).

Continue over Haystacks and past Innominate Tarn, paying your respects to A.W. Pass by Blackbeck Tarn and Little Round How to

Warnscale Beck. Cross this and climb uphill, by quarry spoil, to a mine building at Dubs Quarry. A track goes to the bottom of the dismantled tramway (21000/13400). Follow this to the drum house and down to Honister Pass. (The rails have gone but some sleepers lie by the side.) The area around the quarry buildings is worth exploring. Inside the shop is more old mining machinery. (Once, early one morning on my way down the pass, I got unusually close to a buzzard that was sat on a post.)

At the end of my walk I drove to Buttermere for a drink in the Fish Hotel.

# Walk 30. Black Combe from Beckside

**Map:** OL6; map ref. prefix SD

**Distance:** 22km (14 miles)

**Ascent:** 1120m (3700ft)

**Time:** 9 hours

**Starting point/parking:** Parking area by Beckside Farm, on the A595, 4km NE of Silecroft (152846).

## General description

Often, walkers overlook Black Combe because it isn't easy to involve it in a circular walk of reasonable length. This walk does start and finish at the same place. It goes up the east side of Black Combe, then north to the minor road near Buck Barrow. It returns past the Sunkenkirk (Swinside) stone circle. The finish is along rights of way but these paths can be tricky to follow so, hopefully, this guide will help. Much of the walk is not on recognised paths but, though the ground may be boggy, it isn't difficult. I did this walk, with Jan, on a pleasant day near the end of August.

## Route

On the far side of the road, take a track north for just over 1km, alongside Whitecombe Beck, to Blackcombe Beck (151857). (Spoil from an old copper mine lies nearby.) Jan and I took different routes to the summit of Black Combe.

Jan chose to climb the shoulder to the south of Blackcombe Beck. Although it is steep at first, it isn't too difficult and the way to the top is obvious. Lower down there are tracks through the bracken and there are good views of the coast to the south.

I started on the north side of the beck using a sheep track through the bracken, 20m from the stream. This gives access to the impressive combe below the crags. I climbed the steep slope to the left of the crags, to the summit trig point and shelter (13550/85490, elevation 600m (1970ft)) (1). There ought to have been fabulous views of the

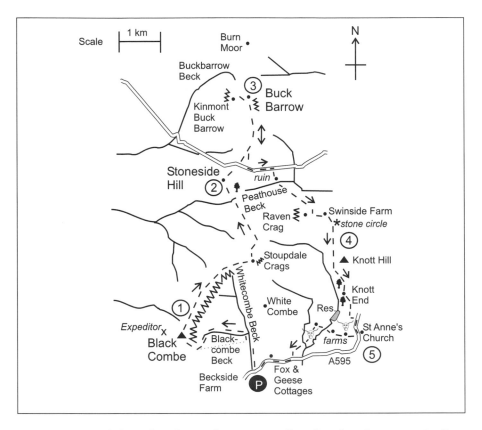

west coast and the Isle of Man but, typically, the clouds swept in five minutes before we got to the top.

Nearby is wreckage from a light transport aircraft, a US Beech C-45 Expeditor that crashed in 1947. It lies 530m away on a bearing of 285° (13045/85651, elevation 515m (1690ft)). The two crew survived blizzards and rain for 18 hours before descending to safety.

From the summit, return to the eastern edge of the screes and go north, then NE along the edge. A path leads down over Hentoe Hill, above Whitecombe Screes, to the top of Whitecombe Beck. Leave the path when it goes down Whitecombe Beck and go to a small cairn above Stoupdale Crags (15150/87370). Walk north to a fence and follow this, northwards for 2.5km to Stoneside Hill. The ground in the dip below the hill was less boggy than I expected. On the OS map there is a stone construction named Charity Chair, but my map

Sunkenkirk stone circle

doesn't show the nearby copse of pine trees. There are good views from the cairn on Stoneside Hill (14590/89270) (2).

Go NE along a path by a wall, to a minor road. If you have time, go 1.5km north to the interesting tors of Buck Barrow (15190/91040, elevation 549m (1799ft)) and Kinmont Buck Barrow (14680/91000, elevation 535m (1754ft)) (3). Return to the minor road and walk east for 800m to a signpost, indicating Swinside 1 mile.

There doesn't appear to be a path, so head 165° over boggy terrain to a ruin by Peathouse Beck (15910/89160). Cross the beck and join a path that goes SE, below Raven Crag. Walk in the direction of a wall that contours below the crag. Keep on the track, which passes Swinside Farm and leads to Sunkenkirk (Swinside) Stone Circle (4). I find this every bit as impressive as Castlerigg Stone Circle.

Continue on the track for 70m to a wall, and then leave it to go south through reeds. Take a path southwards, passing through two walls, on the west side of Knott Hill. The field to the west of the hill is open access so I considered climbing to the trig point, but thick bracken and gorse deterred me. Leave the open access field

(17210/87130). Go south to the wall on your right (17270/86980). Walk along a path by the wall, to the ruins at Knottend. From here, take a track SE, then south and stay on the track, ignoring a stile on the right, to a corner formed by two walls. Go left, to a gap in a wall, and turn right to a junction (17620/85810). Turn left for 100m to a road and right for 250m to a church, St Anne's, Thwaites (5). This had scaffolding and was being repaired.

Opposite the church, over a stile, take a path that goes past Bank House Farm. (The farm's owner said that a right of way was being processed to enable walkers to go directly to the farm from the earlier junction, 17620/85810.) Go over the ladder stile by the farm and stay on the left side of the wall to a stile (17230/85540). (My map indicated going to the right but I couldn't see a way over the wall in the corner. The presence of a bull caused Jan to be a little concerned.) Drop down, west, for 150m, by a fence and ruined wall, (no obvious path) to a stile by Whirlpippin Farm. Turn right, into the farm buildings. A friendly lady, with four dogs, told us that not many walkers came that way; we weren't surprised – there aren't many signposts.

Immediately, opposite the corner of the farm itself, go left through a gate (farm's name on other side). Cross a stream, with the dam wall of Baystone Bank Reservoir in view on the right. Go left at a junction and walk in front of another farm.

The farmer kindly directed us to three metal gates on the left. Through these, go right for 100m to a wooden gate. Take a path, on the left of a wall, that goes to a bridge over the stream. Cross this and go along a track, on the edge of a field (it contained another bull) to the A595. Turn right, past cottages and over a hill, to the car park 800m away. Take care, the traffic is quite fast and there isn't a pavement.

We went to a favourite village, Broughton, for a drink and chose the Manor Arms in the square. It had a good range of beers including Yates, Hawkshead and Timothy Taylors. Afterwards we drove to Morecambe and watched the sun setting close to Black Combe, across Morecambe Bay. I admit to having a soft spot for Morecambe. The views of the Lake District across the sea are as good as any coastal views in England. The seafront is attractive, decorated with birds as a theme, and has a memorial to Eric Morecambe. There is the refurbishment of the art deco Midland Hotel to look forward to.

# Walk 31. Caw Fell and Haycock from Near Thwaites

**Map:** OL4; map ref. prefix NY

**Distance:** 25km (15.5 miles)

**Ascent:** 1060m (3500ft)

**Time:** 9¾ hours

**Starting point/parking:** By the Ennerdale Bridge to Calder Bridge road, 1km south of the Kinniside stone circle. There are spaces for 2 cars by a bend (066130), or by a track off the road leading to Near Thwaites (063131).

## General Description

The walk explores the fells to the west of Ennerdale. Starting from Near Thwaites, it goes to Lank Rigg, Iron Crag, Caw Fell and Haycock. Mostly, it is on good paths, though lower down it is boggy with tussocky grass. There is evidence of early habitation and three aircraft wreck sites may be inspected. My latest visit was on a muggy day in September, with the tops of the hills covered by cloud.

## Route

Take a track that goes eastwards, towards the River Calder, from a bend in the road (066130). Cross the beck that joins the river by a bend, and continue along the track, on the north side of Whoap Beck for a further 1.2km. Cross Whoap Beck and start up the grassy slopes of Lank Rigg (087130) (1). (It is possible to climb directly up Lank Rigg after crossing the river but the terrain is particularly unpleasant. I disturbed a small wading bird in a marshy area by the beck, probably a dunlin.)

Halfway up the hillside, it is possible to find a small amount of wreckage from a Miles Magister trainer that crashed in 1952 (08520/12133 and 08435/12218). The aircraft was on a flight from Blackpool to Carlisle. The pilot survived and walked away from the crash.

The summit of Lank Rigg has a trig point, (09160/11950, elevation 541m (1775ft)). Take a path NE, over the col and up Whoap elevation

CAW FELL · LITTLE GOWDER CRAG · HAYCOCK

Oxford wreckage, Caw Fell

511m (1677ft) (2). From the boulder marking the summit, a path leads NE and swings eastwards towards the wall along the southern side of Ennerdale. When the path peters out, head for the wall as it goes towards the top of Iron Crag (10870/12960). A gate leads to one of several cairns on the other side of the wall (12160/12250).

Some wreckage from a jet fighter aircraft, a Sabre that crashed in 1959 killing the Canadian pilot, has been placed here. Someone has written a few words, in memory of the pilot, on one piece of metal. Continue south for 400m to a cairn marking the highest point on Iron Crag (12320/11920, elevation 642m (2106ft)). To inspect the Sabre crash site and the considerable wreckage, including a wing, go down the western slopes for 400m (12023/11639). From the wreckage, follow a sheep track that contours round to the col below Caw Fell.

Continue up, by the wall as it swings east to Caw Fell. The cairn is just to the north of the wall (13150/10990, elevation 697m (2288ft)) (3). An inverted hanging basket, labelled A, was pegged to the ground

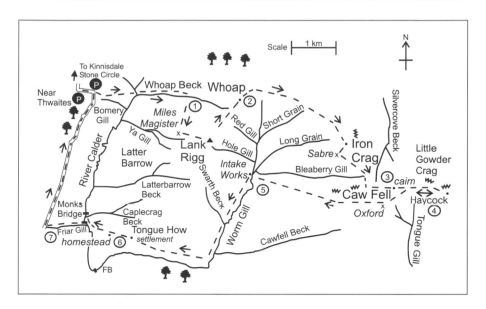

near the cairn; I imagine it was part of an experiment into the effect of sheep grazing.

Although the walk descends from Caw Fell, the opportunity to extend it to visit Haycock should not be missed. Follow the wall for 1km over the rocky tor of Little Gowder Crag (14030/10980, elevation 733m (2405ft)). Continue to the shelter on Haycock. The summit cairn is 40m to the south (14490/10680, elevation 797m (2617ft)) (4).

Return towards Caw Fell, contouring round Little Gowder Crag. At the col before Caw Fell go SW, off-path, down the slope. 100m above the Hanging Stone (marked on OS maps) is wreckage from an aircraft, an Oxford, that crashed in 1941 (13112/10603). The pilot, another Canadian, and another airman were killed.

From the wreckage, contour westwards round Caw Fell then head 290° to the Intake Works by Worm Gill (5). Take the track from these works for 4km to Tongue How. Here, there is evidence of an ancient settlement; particularly impressive is a 10m diameter stone ruin, marked as *homestead* on the map (06990/09870) (6).

Continue down to the bridge over the River Calder. From here, divert 100m north to see an old arched bridge over a gorge. On the map this is named Monks Bridge but Wainwright says it is known locally as Matty Benn's Bridge.

Maps show a right of way along the east side of the river but I wouldn't recommend going this way. Ignore it and return the 100m from Monks Bridge to take the track by Friar Gill to the road (7). It is a 3km walk along the road back to the parking spot. Outside 'going home time' the road isn't too busy and there are grass verges but drivers using it do seem to think they are participating in a rally.

There are two excellent pubs in nearby Ennerdale Bridge: the Fox and Hounds and the Shepherds Arms.

### *Note:*

On my latest visit I descended from Caw Fell and continued SW over Stockdale Moor to explore signs of early habitation there. The walking over the moor isn't difficult with good views of the Scafells, (and less good ones of Calder Hall/Windscale/Sellafield). There is a large collection of stones (10150/07750), various cairns and the temptingly named Sampson's Bratfull, probably a barrow (09840/08050). This visit was a grave error; pardon the pun! The tussocks between there and Worm Gill were purgatory. Also the stream, near the mountain pinfold, isn't easy to cross; after rain it may be impossible, and all to see piles of historical stones!

*Opposite: Thornthwaite Beacon (Walk 33)*

# Section 6: Three Challenges

# Walk 32. A Wastwater Horseshoe

**Maps:** OL4, OL6; map ref. prefix is NY

**Distance:** 32.5km (20.5 miles)

**Ascent:** 2560m (8400ft)

**Time:** 14½ hours

**Starting point/parking:** There are spaces near the road junction, by the point marked on OS maps as a 'landing stage', on the NW side of Wast Water (151053).

---

## General Description

A few years ago, Tony and I tried a route that started: Middle Fell, Seatallan, Haycock, Scoat Fell, Pillar, Kirk Fell and down to Beck Head. With Great Gable ahead, Tony suggested a detour for a pint in the Wastwater Head Inn! Afterwards, we finished along the eastern side of the lake, below The Screes. It was a kind of horseshoe, but not quite the one we'd planned.

For the walk I describe here, I was alone and decided to go anti-clockwise. I didn't want to go the obvious way, over all the main peaks: Scafell, Scafell Pike, Scoat Fell, Haycock etc. I wished to spend some time away from popular paths. I chose to walk above The Screes and to pass below Scafell. I took the Corridor Route to Sty Head and could see little alternative to going over Great Gable, Kirk Fell and Pillar. For an unusual finish I went to Red Pike, dropped down to Scoat Tarn and contoured round the top of Nether Beck to get to Greendale Tarn. There are many possible variations for you to choose from. For my walk it was cloudy and clammy.

## Route

Walk SW along the road by Wast Water. Where the road leaves the lake, continue on the lakeside path (148048). Go through Low Wood to Lund Bridge (142039). Turn left over the bridge for 300m. A gate is reached, but don't go through it. (I made the mistake of taking a path through chest-high bracken signed-posted "TO THE FELLS". My clothes got soaked and took ages to dry out.) Go sharp right along a track. After 120m, turn left along a path by a wall heading towards the hillside. This path leads to a stile (14280/03530).

Climb steeply up the path, east of Greathall Gill. When I was there, bags of stones had been dropped by helicopter, so this may be a nice stairway by now. At the top of the slope turn left to Whin Rigg (15120/03470) (1). Continue NE on a good path for 2.5km to Illgill Head (16900/04950). A thin path drops, on a bearing of 060°, to the high point of the Corpse Road (from Wasdale Head to Boot) (18360/05560).

To the south is Burnmoor Tarn, which has the third largest surface area of tarns in the Lake District. Also, 200m from the high point, is the grandly named Maiden Castle. This has been reduced to a circular ring of stones with a cairn in the middle (184054).

Go NE across boggy ground and steeply up tussocky grass to the gash of Groove Gill. 200m further, the path to Scafell is met. My idea was to go to the top of Black Crag and try to contour round into Hollow Stones. (A better choice may be to contour round below Black Crag, rather than above it). I left the path at 201067 and went to the top of Black Crag (20280/06890) (2). I saw a path going right and followed it past a cairn thinking it looked promising! It may be a climber's path, because I had to descend steeply down a nasty gully to reach Hollow Stones. (It would be better to accept the loss of height and drop down the scree immediately, from the top of Black Crag to Hollow Stones.) Go north across Hollow Stones, to a main path from Wasdale to Scafell Pike (205074). Walk up this for 800m, until you are close to the top of Piers Gill (21090/07700).

On one walk, Tony and I stopped here for a rest. He took out our packed lunch, prepared by the landlady at Burnthwaite where we'd had B&B the night before, forgot about it and left it there. I only hope someone found it and enjoyed it, particularly the cake. I pulled Tony's leg about this so much that he actually wrote to the landlady and she sent a replacement cake, which he presented to me on a special occasion.

Go NE, dropping down to the Corridor Route and the top of the Piers Gill. Take the Corridor Route to Sty Head. Don't take the path down the gully before Stand Crag, but go above the crag (21900/08470). Along here, I began to be overtaken by fell runners. I

Wast Water

remembered that the first Saturday of August is the date of the
Borrowdale Fell Race (see Walk 4). I followed the runners as they cut
across from Spout Head (221092), to the checkpoint by the stretcher
box at Sty Head (3). At least they had the decency to walk, rather than
run past me as I plodded up to the summit of Great Gable
(21100/10320, elevation 899m (2949ft)). Near the cairn is The Fell &
Rock Club memorial to its members who were killed in the First
World War.

On one occasion, I met a man who had saved Great Gable for the
last of his 'Wainwrights'. His friends formed a guard of honour with
their walking poles. Unfortunately he asked me to use his
new-fangled digital camera to photograph the event and I fear that I
may have botched the recording of this memorable occasion.

Take the steep and rocky path NW from the summit. Make sure to
turn to the west near the bottom, to go to Beckhead Tarn
(20510/10700). In the mist, I found myself on a path to Ennerdale and

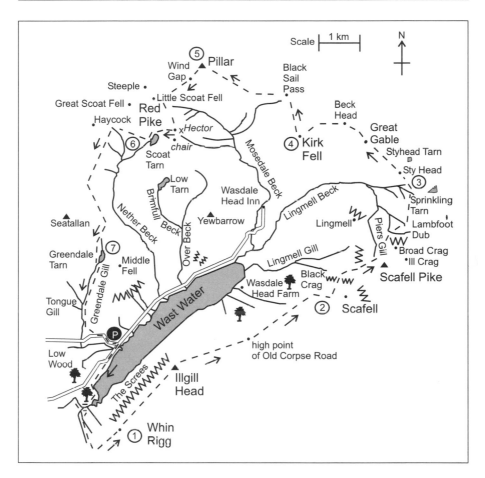

spent some time making my way round the NW corner of Great Gable. From Beck Head the route is straightforward: to Kirk Fell over a lower cairn then the higher one (19490/10480, elevation 802m (2630ft)) (4); followed by Black Sail Pass; Pillar (17120/12100, elevation 892m (2927ft)) (5); Wind Gap and Black Crag. I took a path that contours below Scoat Fell to Red Pike (16530/10610, elevation 826m (2709ft)).

From Red Pike I went west, finding a way between the crags, to join the path by the beck that feeds into Scoat Tarn, a lovely, quiet place. One obvious way to finish would be by Nether Beck. My route was to contour west, then NW around the higher part of Nether Beck (151105) (6). I walked along the gentle slope below Haycock and headed southwards to the boggy hollow, near the spot marked Pots of Ashness on OS maps. Across the hollow, I took a path that passes to the east of Seatallan (starts at 14590/09030). This path swings towards Middle Fell and where it rises, I took a faint path to the right (14860/08070). This leads to the west side of the delightful Greendale Tarn (7). A good path goes from the tarn to Greendale Farm. At the farm turn left down to the lake and car park.

There are two inns in Nether Wasdale, the Screes and the Strands, and three more good pubs at Gosforth.

### *Notes:*

In 1941 a Hawker Hector biplane crashed into the cliffs below Red Pike. There is still a lot of wreckage at the site including the engine. I have managed to get there from the summit ridge but it isn't easy. (I did have the bonus of seeing a ring ouzel). The wreckage lies on a flat section and is marked by a cross, made from metal struts (16750/10375). Another feature on Red Pike is The Chair, made from rocks at the southern end of the ridge from Red Pike (16550/10050).

In April we stayed at the Murt camping barn with the aim of climbing Pillar Rock to complete Tony L's Lakes 2000'ers. There was too much snow for this, so we did a circuit above Mosedale. At Dore Head I met a fell runner, Alison Weston, who told me that she was practising for the Bob Graham Round (42 peaks and approx. 72 miles in less than 24 hours!). She successfully completed the run in May 2006 and was awarded Ilkley Harriers Runner of the Month.

# Walk 33. Wasdale Head (east) to Wasdale Head (west)

**Maps:** OL5, OL6, OL7; map ref. prefix is NY

**Distance:** 48km (30 miles)

**Ascent:** 2900m (9500ft)

**Time:** 20 hours (Generous, I think 15 hours is a reasonable target)

**Starting point/parking:** Lay-by at the summit of the A6 over the Shap Fells (553062). (At the end of the lay-by, there is a memorial to the drivers and locals who suffered the winter conditions on the old Shap road before the M6 was built.)

## General Description

In fact this doesn't quite start at Wasdale Head, but I couldn't resist the title. The Shap Pink Quarry road has no public access, making it difficult to get to Wasdale Head. Hence, the start is slightly to the south. I chose to use mountain passes to cross the Lake District from east to west. Unfortunately, I left this walk until October, which only gave me 12 hours of daylight. This meant I had to hurry and couldn't fully enjoy the scenery.

The walk has similarities to Ken Wilson's 42-mile, Shap to Ravenglass walk in *The Big Walks*. I did that one with Dave, some years ago, but took a route further to the south than on the Wasdale Head walk. On the Ravenglass walk, at Ore Gap by Bowfell, I recall the question "How's it going?" being answered with "The good news, it's all downhill from here: the bad news, 16 miles to go".

## Route

On the west side of the road, go over a gate and take the track along the fence to What Shaw. (Incidentally, this hill completes the 1500ft'ers on this ridge in the Wet Sleddale walk (see walk 24).)

Continue along the fence, boggy in places, to Little Yarlside. (On the way I flushed out a small wader, probably a dunlin, and a few grouse. An American F-111 crashed here in 1975 (see Walk 24).) Follow the wall up to Great Yarlside, trig point by the wall

KIRK FELL    GREAT GABLE    GREEN GABLE

Sprinkling Tarn

(52550/07590) (1). Continue by the fence, on good ground, to Harrop Pike. The fences in this walk detract from the feeling of isolation but are helpful when visibility is poor.

From the large cairn on Harrop Pike, head on a bearing of 250°, to the fence that rises to Tarn Crag. (I saw five deer near Greycrag Tarn.) Follow the path to Tarn Crag and then go northwards along the fence to the col below Branstree. I decided to leave the path and contour round to the top of Gatescarth Pass. A path starts in that direction but turns downhill. The rest of the way across is horrible so including Branstree would have been pleasanter and not taken much extra time.

Crossing this Slough of Despond, the clouds came down and it started to rain. It had taken two hours to reach Gatescarth Pass, a low point in both meanings of the phrase (2).

Follow the good path over Adam Seat to Harter Fell. The start of the descent to Nan Bield Pass is marked by a cairn 130m from the summit, on a bearing of 260°.

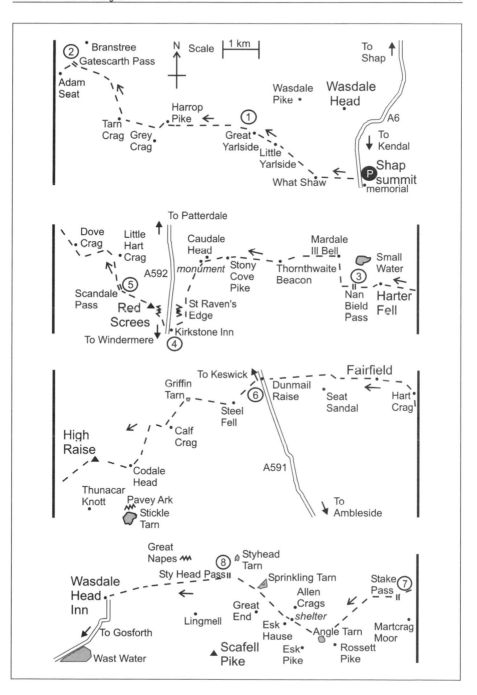

In cloud, I lost time locating the path, but I did get a view of Haweswater from the shelter at Nan Bield Pass (3). Go NW towards Mardale Ill Bell but just before, take a path left (44840/09870). This swings westwards and after 900m take a right fork (44000/10270). High Street is crossed (43650/10190), and the path goes SW towards the magnificent beacon at Thornthwaite Crag. The beacon is 14 feet high and a memorial to a Hugh Roberts has been placed in it. Take a path that starts northwards to Threshthwaite Mouth. It drops steeply to the col and then goes up Threshthwaite Crag, by a wall. (Deer often roam on the slopes to the north, above Hayeswater.) Go over Stony Cove Pike to Caudale Moor. Make a brief diversion to a memorial to Mark Atkinson, a former landlord of the Kirkstone Pass Inn. A plaque with his son's name, William, has been added (41205/09888). Continue southwards along the wall to St Raven's Edge and go west down to Kirkstone Pass (4). (I tried to save time by cutting diagonally to the road; it's not worth it!).

> 'This block – and yon, whose Church-like frame
> Gives to the savage Pass its name'
>
> *Wordsworth, from 'Ode to the Pass of Kirkstone'*

Cross the road and, from near the car park, a good path goes up to the top of Red Screes (39650/08760, elevation 776m (2546ft)). (This is about halfway, and had taken me 5 hours 10 minutes.)

Take a grassy path west and go down 400m to a wall. Follow this down to Scandale Pass (5). Continue past Little Hart Crag and along a fence, westwards, over Bakestones Moss to gain the main ridge to Dove Crag. Walk along a good path by a fence over Dove Crag and Hart Crag and continue to Fairfield. At the shelter, several people on the Fairfield Horseshoe were having problems finding the path to Hart Crag (35860/11720). I hope I helped by indicating the direction I had come from. I went westwards off Fairfield, but it was my turn to have difficulties finding a path. The size of the top of Fairfield, plus several cairns, make life difficult. The cliffs to the east are dangerous and people have been killed in winter conditions. Eventually, I found the path to Hause Gap and took the path across the flank of Seat Sandal. To the west of Grisedale Tarn, a path goes down by the side of Raise

Beck to Dunmail Raise, the highest point of the A591 (6). (My time was now 7 hours 10 minutes.)

The cairn between the carriageways is supposed to be the burial site of Dunmail, a king of Cumbria. Cross the road and step over a fence on the far side. I went to the right of a fence that climbs directly up Steel Fell, up a steep and slippery grass tongue. Towards the top, I rejoined the fence and went up to a cairn (32200/11690). Follow the fence southwards to the top of Steel Fell (31940/11150).

The fence continues west to an unnamed tarn (30760/11140). A. Harry Griffin, who wrote a column for *The Guardian*, often remarked on its lack of name. It has been suggested that it should be named Griffin Tarn. Keep by the fence as is meanders SW to Codale Head. The fence just consists of old posts and in the mist I lost it a couple of times. Go west to the summit of High Raise. (My time so far was 9 hours 15 minutes.) From a cairn to the south, a path starts SW to Stake Beck (A point on the path is 27500/09160.) Cross Stake Beck to the Stake Pass path, aiming for a point by a small tarn (26500/087500) (7)

Take a path west, then SW behind Black Crags and Rossett Pike to Angle Tarn. I lost the path and floundered around on awful terrain. (I nearly trod on a wader; from the white rump and wing markings I think it was another dunlin.) After falling in the mire a couple of times, I found a path that led to the tarn. As the sun disappeared, the weather suddenly cleared to give good views. The main path goes up two slopes to Esk Hause. It descends past Sprinkling Tarn, where I exchanged pleasantries with a camper and his dog, to Sty Head (8). Along this path, two needles may be seen on the side of Great Gable. I think the lower one is Napes Needle.

The light faded as I stumbled down the stony path to the Wasdale Head Inn and it was dark when I arrived, 12 hours after the start. I probably spent an hour or more of this time stopping to check my position and work out directions. It would be more sensible and enjoyable to do this walk on a summer's day or even to split it over two days.

If more time were available, it would be tempting to have lunch at the Kirkstone Pass Inn and also visit the Brothers Parting Stone, where William Wordsworth last saw his brother John on 29/09/1800. John drowned when his ship *The Earl of Abergavenny* sank in

Weymouth Bay. The rock is well marked with a sign, just to the SE of the path to Patterdale, near Grisedale Tarn. The words, now illegible, are:

> 'Here did we stop; and here looked round
> While each into himself descends,
> For that last thought of parting Friends
> That is not to be found.
> Brother and friend, if verse of mine
> Have power to make thy virtues known,
> Here let a monumental Stone
> Stand – sacred as a Shrine.'

# Walk 34. A Langdale Horseshoe

**Maps:** OL6; map ref. prefix is NY

**Distance:** 13.5km (8.5 miles)

**Ascent:** 400m (1300ft)

**Time:** 8 hours. This route will be most appreciated in the afternoon and evening.

**Starting point/parking:** Elterwater. There is a bus service between Ambleside and the Old Dungeon Ghyll Hotel. Alternatively, there is space for several cars in Elter Water (33333/04200).

## General description

The route takes in two valleys: Great Langdale and Little Langdale. It should be on good paths and roads. It would suit a day when the weather conditions are poor. The main features are tarns and historic buildings.

## Route

From the centre of Elterwater, take the road south over the bridge across Great Langdale Beck. On the right is our first historic building, the Britannia Inn; this should be given a close inspection (1). When you exit the building, continue past the Youth Hostel and after 200m turn right, off the main road. Go along a track for a further 200m and take a left fork, uphill past disused quarries. The sewage works to the left should be avoided.

Continue on the track to Little Langdale and, 2km from Elterwater, a road is met at a T-junction (31370/03480). Turn left and after 400m another historic building should be visited, the Three Shires Inn (2). (The Three Shires were Lancashire, Westmorland and Cumberland. The Three Shires Stone near the top of Wrynose Pass commemorates the point where they met.)

Leave the building and walk westwards along the road, with a view of Little Langdale Tarn to the south. At a road junction, turn right towards Blea Tarn (30160/03350). Notice the distinctive tor of Castle Howe, near Fell Foot. 1km from the junction, turn left along a

The Britannia

path that passes to the south of Blea Tarn. After 300m take the path that goes along the western side of the tarn. This leads to the road near Side Pike. (There is the opportunity to test one's girth by climbing up Side Pike via Fat Man's Agony (see Walk 14).)

Turn left down the road towards Great Langdale. Go over a stile on the right and then go left, along a footpath that goes through the NT campsite, to the Old Dungeon Ghyll Hotel (3). This establishment has a good display of climbing photographs that should not be missed.

From here, walk eastwards, either along the road or the right of way from the pub car park, for 1km to the Sticklebarn Tavern (4). After looking at the interior of this building, or sitting at the tables outside, scramble 50m east to the New Dungeon Ghyll Hotel (5).

After visiting this historic building, return *past* the Sticklebarn Tavern, go through the NT car park and cross the road to a footpath. This goes through a field and over Great Langdale Beck, to Side House. Turn east, along the Cumbria Way and follow this for 3km to a

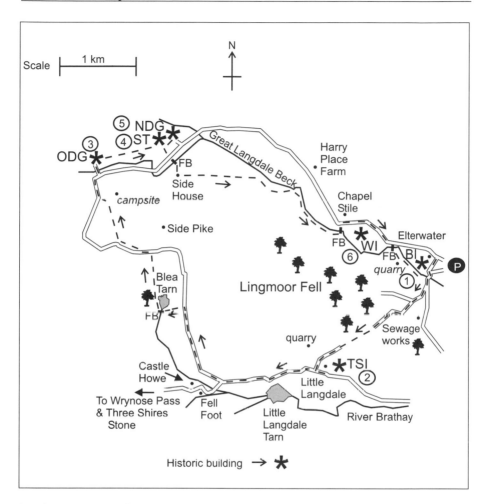

bridge, New Bridge. Cross it and go to Chapel Stile. (By the road 500m north of Chapel Stile is (A) Harry (Griffin) Place Farm.)

Walk through this lovely village to yet another historic building on the right, Wainwrights' Inn (the inn sign shows a man working on a cartwheel; an alternative might be the head of a man with a pipe) (6).

The walk could end here but the perfectionist, with time (and money) to spare may wish to complete this circular walk by returning to Elterwater to partake of further refreshment. It has been suggested that a (still) capable walker might complete more than one lap of the circuit.

# *Appendix*

## Aircraft Wreck Sites

I have used a GPS to record the map references. In many cases there is very little wreckage and the usual six-figure reference is not accurate enough to locate the site easily. Hence I have given the GPS ten figure reference. This should lead you to within 10 metres or so of the site.

For example, from the first line of the table: 21497/10663. The 21497 is the easting and 10663 the northing. The equivalent 6-fig. ref. would be 214106. However, this gives a 100m square to search.

This is not a comprehensive list of Lakeland crash sites, only the ones I have visited. Some crash sites have memorial plaques. It would be fitting if all the aircrew that died in wartime accidents in Lakeland were commemorated in this way. Also, it might create more respect for the sites and discourage people from removing pieces of wreckage.

| Aircraft | Crash Date | Place | 10-fig map ref | Amount | Walk |
|---|---|---|---|---|---|
| Avro Anson | 09/08/1943 | Green Gable | NY 21497/10663 | S | 1 |
| Avro Anson | 09/08/1943 | Scafell | NY 20845/06170 | M | 12 & 18 |
| Avro Anson | 30/01/1944 | Starling Dodd | NY 14208/15740 | E | 28 |
| Avro Anson | 20/03/1944 | Swirl How | NY 27763/00143 | M | 13 |
| Dominie | 30/08/1946 | Broad Crag | NY 21720/07755 | M | 12 |
| Expeditor | 12/03/1947 | Black Combe | SD 13045/85651 | M | 30 |
| Halifax | 24/01/1944 | Eel Crag | NY 19358/20369 | M | 7 |
| Halifax | 22/10/1944 | Great Carrs | NY 27004/00811 | L | 16 |
| Hawker Hector | 08/09/1941 | Red Pike | NY 16750/10375 | M | 32 |
| Hurricane | 31/03/1941 | Scar Crags | NY 21023/20691 | E | 7 |
| Hurricane | 12/08/1941 | Slight Side | NY 20850/05040 | M | 18 |
| Hurricane | 12/08/1941 | Slight Side | NY 20810/05165 | M | 18 |
| Hurricane | 23/04/1943 | Brim Fell | SD 27139/98873 | S | 13 |
| Lockheed Hudson | 10/11/1942 | Beda Fell | NY 42700/17086 | E | 25 |
| Miles Magister | 22/07/1952 | Lank Rigg | NY 08520/12133 | E | 31 |
| Mosquito | 10/02/1945 | Striding Edge | NY 34880/15132 | E | 19 |
| Oxford | 02/11/1941 | Caw Fell | NY 13112/10603 | M | 31 |
| Piper Saratoga | 29/11/1987 | Bowfell | NY 24504/06268 | M | 15 |
| Spitfire | 20/11/1947 | Ill Crag | NY 22505/07714 | E | 5 & 18 |
| Sabre | 26/06/1959 | Iron Crag | NY 12023/11639 | L | 31 |
| Vildebeeste | 04/06/1937 | Crinkle Crags | NY 25075/05170 | E | 14 |
| Wellington | 16/06/1944 | Red Pike | NY 15987/15803 | S | 28 |

**Amount of wreckage:** L – Considerable; M – Medium; S – Small; E – Extremely small

The following books provide further information, although some of the map references are inaccurate:

*Air Crashes in the Lake District* – Michael J. Hurst

*High Ground Wrecks and Relics* – David J. Smith

*Hell on High Ground Vols. 1 & 2* – David W. Earl

### Useful websites:

Rich Allenby's site: www.allenby.info_

Alan Clark's www.peakdistrictaircrashes.co.uk (links to the Lake District)

# *Also of Interest*

## DARK PEAK HIKES:
### *off the beaten track*
### *Doug Brown*

Also by the author of "Lakeland Hikes", this companion book covers The Dark Peak area of the Peak District: a landscape of steep slopes, gritstone crags and peat moorlands. Doug offers a collection of 34 routes for those who enjoy the challenge of using their navigational skills for route finding and locating items of interest. These include: sites of aircraft wrecks; memorials; Bronze Age barrows; Iron Age forts; and remnants of an industrial past. Joe Brown's map-reading trail is included, following clues chiselled into walls, bridges and gateposts. *£7.95*

## WALKING THE WAINWRIGHTS
### *Stuart Marshall*

This book links all 214 peaks in the late Alfred Wainwright's seven-volume *Pictorial Guide to The Lakeland Fells*. Route descriptions are clearly presented with two-colour sketch maps. "An excellent, concise manual on how to tackle the 'Wainwrights' in an intelligent way." – A. Harry Griffin MBE *£8.95*

## WATERSIDE WALKS IN THE LAKE DISTRICT
### *Colin Shelbourn*

25 stunning waterside walks alongside the lakes, tarns, becks, rivers and waterfalls of the Lake District. Choose from a short stroll to a 16km (10ml) circular walk around the Queen of the Lakes, Derwent Water. Whatever the length or location you choose you'll meet with stunning scenery, a richness of wildlife, and many interesting places to visit, often a welcome distraction from the rudiments of pure walking. *£7.95*

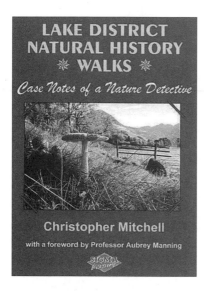

## WALKS IN ANCIENT LAKELAND

*Robert Harris*

Discover stone circles, standing stones and burial cairns decorating these beautiful hills. Follow ancient trackways and explore remote areas to uncover the mysteries of the lives of our ancestors. Accurate sketch maps guide you to sites in valleys or the wild and remote fells. Intricate hand-drawn sketches depict the standing stones and circles raised in the past by our Lake District ancestors. *£6.95*

## LAKE DISTRICT NATURAL HISTORY WALKS: Case Notes of a Nature Detective

*Christopher Mitchell*

Walks for all ages and abilities, encouraging you to look at the countryside in a different way. At every turn, you find a world of plant and animal signs. Fascinating facts help you interpret the countryside by looking at the effects of geology and plant life on the animal population of the area. **Winner of the 2005 Outdoor Writers' Guild 'Book of The Year (Guidebook category)' awards** *£8.95*

## WALKING IN EDEN: 2nd Edition

*Ron Scholes*

This is an updated collection of linear and circular walks in the Eden Valley, close to the Lake District. There are villages and the traditional towns of Penrith, Appleby, Kirkby Stephen and Alston to explore, plus a wonderful variety of walks. Ron Scholes guides you through this forgotten wilderness in 30 circular and direct walks. *£8.95*

All of our books are available through booksellers. In case of difficulty, or for a free catalogue, please contact:

**SIGMA LEISURE, 5 ALTON ROAD, WILMSLOW, CHESHIRE SK9 5DY**
**Phone:** *01625-531035* **E-mail:** *info@sigmapress.co.uk*
**Web site:** *www.sigmapress.co.uk*